PAUL
THE APOSTLE
GRAPHIC STORY BIBLE

BEN AVERY   MARK HARMON

MARIO DEMATTEO

MARK HARMON

ILLUSTRATOR / COLORIST / LETTERER

BRETT BURNER

PRODUCER / ASSISTANT EDITOR

MARCOS MUJICA

BIBLE CONSULTANT

BroadStreet Publishing® Group, LLC
Savage, Minnesota, USA
BroadStreetPublishing.com

Paul the Apostle: Graphic Story Bible

Copyright © 2019 Beartruth Collective, LLC

No part of this publication may be reproduced, distributed, or transmitted in any form or by any means, including photocopying, recording, or other electronic or mechanical methods, without the prior written permission of the publisher. For information regarding permission, email info@broadstreetpublishing.com.

Scripture quotations are taken from the Holy Bible, New Living Translation, copyright ©1996, 2004, 2007, 2013 by Tyndale House Foundation. Used by permission of Tyndale House Publishers, Inc., Carol Stream, Illinois 60188. All rights reserved.

9781424558995

Printed in China

Paul the Apostle is an engaging and contemporary take on a towering figure in both Christianity and the history of the Western world. Crisply drawn and compulsively readable, this graphic novel takes readers on a journey that is sometimes dark and often humorous. Supporting Scripture references are discretely placed, making this an appealing read for history buffs, graphic novel fans, and believers. I loved it!

—**LYNN VINCENT**, #1 *New York Times* bestselling author of *Heaven is for Real* and *Same Kind of Different as Me*

When I read *Paul the Apostle*, it brought the whole story of Paul to life in such a unique way. It left me in tears. I highly recommend it!

—**KATIE LEIGH**, voice actress for *Adventures in Odyssey*

This is a wonderful blend of historical and Biblical accuracy in a futuristic comic book. My kids keep going back to it!

—**DR. SHAWN BEATY**, senior pastor

Young students can appreciate an exciting plot and fun characters, while older students and adults can recognize the nuances, symbols, and themes that bring out Biblical truths.

—**ABBY BARRANTES**, youth director

I love *Paul the Apostle* because it points kids to the Bible. Whenever you can bring the Bible alive and get students interested in reading it on their own, it's a big win!

—**SCOTT PITTMAN**, middle school pastor

I recently had the privilege of using *Paul the Apostle* in my sixth-grade classroom. As a teacher of forty-one years, I was extremely excited and pleased with the enthusiastic reaction my students showed toward the book. They were instantly engaged from the beginning because it is a graphic novel. Even my reluctant readers found it very difficult to put the book down.

—**MS. PEGGY COUGHLIN**, teacher

I loved *Paul the Apostle* so much. I already read it once and plan on reading it 100 more times. Barnabas was my favorite character. He's so cute and loves his friend Paul with his super big heart.

—**ALEXIS**, 8 years old

THANKS FOR CHECKING OUT *PAUL THE APOSTLE*.

A FEW YEARS AGO, WE WERE READING OUR FAVORITE COMIC BOOKS AND WONDERED HOW COOL IT WOULD BE TO MAKE A GRAPHIC STORY BIBLE WITH AWESOME LOOKING CARTOON CREATURES, SET IN A FUTURISTIC UNIVERSE. IT WAS A PRETTY FAR-OUT IDEA. WITH MUCH PRAYER AND COUNSEL, WE DECIDED TO TAKE A LEAP OF FAITH. IN YOUR HANDS IS THE FIRST INSTALLMENT OF OUR FUTURISTIC GRAPHIC STORY BIBLE COME TO LIFE.

OUR INTENTION HAS ALWAYS BEEN ONE OF MINISTRY AND EDUCATION. WE'RE USING FUTURISTIC GRAPHIC NOVEL LANGUAGE TO ILLUMINATE THE STORY OF PAUL THE APOSTLE AND, ULTIMATELY, THE LIFE-TRANSFORMING MESSAGE OF JESUS CHRIST. IN NO WAY ARE WE TRYING TO REPLACE THE BIBLE OR ENHANCE IT. THE WORD OF GOD IS ALREADY AWESOME AND PERFECT! FOR THIS REASON, WE STRIVE FOR OUR ADAPTATION TO BE AN ACCURATE PORTRAYAL OF THE BIBLICAL ACCOUNT. WE'VE INCLUDED SCRIPTURAL REFERENCES AT THE BOTTOM OF PAGES THROUGHOUT THE BOOK TO INSPIRE READERS TO CHECK OUT WHERE ALL THIS AWESOMENESS ACTUALLY COMES FROM— THE BIBLE!

PROLOGUE

WHEN THE ROMANS HUNG JESUS OF NAZARETH ON THE CROSS TO DIE, THEY EXPECTED HIM TO REMAIN IN THE GRAVE. BUT HE ROSE AGAIN, HAVING DEFEATED DEATH, AND IGNITED A REVOLUTIONARY MOVEMENT OF SALVATION. THE ROMANS COULD NEVER HAVE SUSPECTED THAT EXECUTING JESUS WAS ALL PART OF GOD'S DIVINE PLAN FOR CREATION. FOR FORTY DAYS, THE RISEN JESUS MET WITH HIS FOLLOWERS, PREPARING THEM FOR THE PERSECUTION THEY WOULD FACE AFTER HE LEFT THE EARTH. HE SPOKE OF WHEN HE WOULD RETURN AS THE RIGHTFUL KING OF ALL CREATION. THE MOVEMENT JESUS STARTED, KNOWN AS "THE WAY," SPREAD OVER THE LAND LIKE WILDFIRE. THIS IS THE STORY OF ONE OF HIS BRAVE FOLLOWERS WHO HELPED SPREAD THE MESSAGE.

CHAPTER ONE:
THE CHOSEN

"FOR I CAN DO EVERYTHING THROUGH CHRIST, WHO GIVES ME STRENGTH."

-PHILIPPIANS 4:13 (NLT)

¹1 TIMOTHY 1:2 (NLT)

THE REVOLUTION HAS ONLY JUST BEGUN.

GREETINGS! I'M HERE TO SEE THE PRISONER PAUL.

YOU AGAIN?

THAT'S RIGHT.

ME AGAIN.

YOU'RE ONE PERSISTENT LIL' FELLA!

IT'S GONNA COST YOU A FULL DENARIUS.

BUT THAT'S A FULL DAY'S WAGES!

TAKE IT OR LEAVE IT, CHRISTIAN SCUM!

GIVE TO CAESAR WHAT IS CAESAR'S.

RECEIVING

P.I.M CONNECTED

BZZZT

BZZZT

P.I.M. CONNECTED
TRANSFERING.
DENARIOUS I

DENARIOUS

P.I.M DECONNECTED
TRANSACTION COMPLETE

NOT SO FAST!

BUT I JUST GAVE YOU A DAY'S WAGES.

CAN'T HAVE YOU SMUGGLE IN A WEAPON OR SOMETHING...

...EVEN IF YOU RELIGIOUS IDIOTS *ARE* PACIFISTS.

HMMM. SOUP.

YOU HAVEN'T MET PETER...

CAN'T BREAK OUT OF NERO'S PRISON WITH SOUP!

ONLY WAY ANYONE LEAVES THIS PLACE IS ON THE CHOPPING BLOCK, AS FOOD FOR LIONS, OR ON A CROSS!

HAVE A NICE DAY!

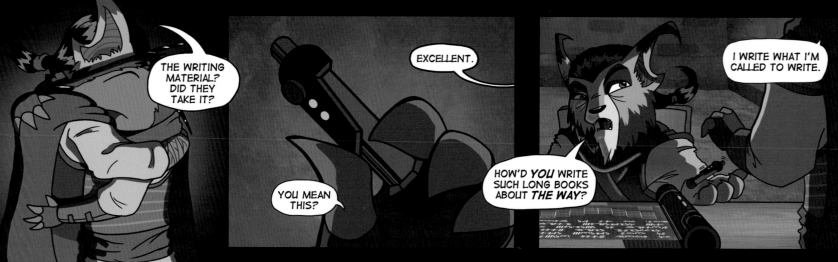

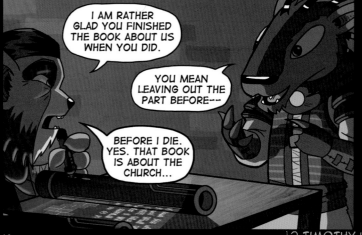

[1] 2 TIMOTHY 4:21 (NLT), [2] 2 TIMOTHY 4:18 (NLT)

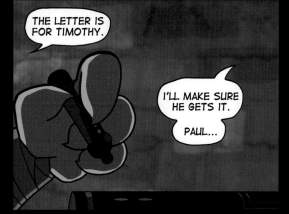

...WITH A DIFFERENT NAME.

SAUL?

HOW COULD YOU?!?

JERUSALEM, 35 A.D.

YOU CONVINCED THE SANHEDRIN TO LET THOSE JESUS-FOLLOWERS GO!

YOU'VE SAID THAT WE WILL TOLERATE THIS CULT IN OUR MIDST!

YOUR ACTIONS WEAKEN OUR ENTIRE BELIEF SYSTEM!!!

YOU'VE SET A PRECEDENT, GAMALIEL!

IF I SPEAK, SAUL, WILL YOU LISTEN OR JUST SHOUT ME DOWN?

SPEAK!

BUT I DON'T KNOW WHAT YOU COULD POSSIBLY SAY FOR YOURSELF.

I SPOKE FOR MYSELF AT THE TRIAL.

NOW YOU WANT PERMISSION TO HUNT THE FOLLOWERS OF THE CARPENTER...

SAUL, WHEN DID YOUR PASSION BECOME SUCH WRATH?

YOU ARE NO LONGER MY INSTRUCTOR.

THEY WERE ARRESTED FOR SPREADING THAT LUNATIC'S TEACHINGS!

AND MERELY SLAPPED ON THE WRIST!

BUT THOSE TEACHINGS ARE A THREAT TO OUR VERY WAY OF LIFE!

FOR A WAY OF LIFE TO BE THREATENED BY ONE MAN'S TEACHINGS...

...IT IS EITHER A WEAK WAY OF LIFE...

...OR SOME VERY STRONG TEACHINGS.

THE SANHEDRIN WANTED TO MAKE MARTYRS OUT OF THOSE MEN, SAUL!

THOSE MEN TRULY BELIEVE WHAT THEY ARE TEACHING!

BUT IF WHAT THEY BELIEVE IS A LIE, IT WILL BLOW AWAY IN THE WINDS OF TIME LIKE DUST!

YES, THEY ARE FOOLS TO FOLLOW JESUS!

BUT IF WE HAD KILLED THEM, THE TROUBLES WOULD HAVE BEEN MULTIPLIED!

THEY *HAVE* MULTIPLIED!

THEY SPREAD LIKE FILTHY RATS!

SLAM!

BUT THIS WAS BEYOND ROMAN LAW, WAS IT NOT?

AND OUT OF THE SANHEDRIN'S HANDS.

THERE'S ONLY ONE WAY TO END THIS.

HERE, LET ME HELP YOU.

HIS SIN IS AGAINST GOD AND GOD'S PEOPLE.

ACTS 7:58-60

...I COULD BE A SPECTATOR NO LONGER.

THE TIME, TEACHERS, IS NOW! AND I AM THE ONE TO DO IT.

MY DEVOTION TO OUR WAYS AND OUR GOD CANNOT BE DISPUTED.

NEITHER CAN THE THREAT THESE PEOPLE POSE TO OUR WAYS.

BUT THESE PEOPLE CANNOT POSSIBLY POSE A THREAT TO OUR GOD.

THESE FOOLS DISOBEY YOUR COMMANDS, ESCAPE OUR PRISONS, AND PREACH THEIR LIES.

GOD USES THE HANDS OF MEN TO DO HIS WORK. DAVID AND THE GIANT. MOSES AND THE EXODUS. JOSHUA AND JERICHO.

THIS IS MY CALLING.

YOU PUT YOURSELF IN DISTINGUISHED COMPANY!

BUT, LIKE YOU, EACH OF THOSE MEN HAD A CALLING TO SERVE GOD AND SERVE HIS PEOPLE.

I SEE THAT IN YOU, SAUL.

WHAT HAPPENED TODAY CANNOT HAPPEN AGAIN.

MAKING STEPHEN A MARTYR ADDS TO THEIR RESOLVE!

WE GIVE YOU PERMISSION TO HUNT THEM DOWN AND ARREST THEM. BUT BRING THEM HERE FOR JUDGMENT!

YOU CAN TRUST ME, HIGH PRIEST!

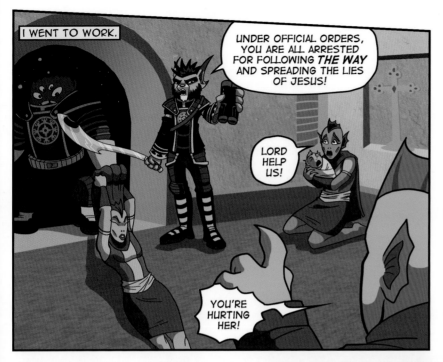

FATHER GOD, GUIDE ME ON THIS MISSION.

I AM YOURS, LORD.

SAUL?

I HAVE HEARD OF YOUR NEW REQUEST TO THE COUNCIL.

THE FOLLOWERS OF *THE WAY* HAVE BEEN RUN OUT OF JERUSALEM.

BUT, AS THEY RUN, THEY SPREAD THEIR TEACHINGS!

THEY MUST BE STOPPED.

AND SO, YOU BELIEVE HUNTING THEM DOWN IS WHAT GOD WOULD HAVE YOU DO ABOUT IT?

I SEEK GOD'S WISDOM, HIS RIGHTEOUSNESS, AND HIS DIVINE WILL.

GOING TO DAMASCUS TO SEEK OUT THE FOLLOWERS OF THE DEAD CARPENTER IS WHAT HE WANTS ME TO DO.

I HAVE WRITTEN ORDERS FROM THE HIGH PRIEST TO ARREST ANY FOLLOWERS OF JESUS IN DAMASCUS.

SAUL, WHEN YOU *TRULY* SEEK THE WILL OF GOD, BE READY FOR *HIM* TO REVEAL IT.

IF THIS ISN'T GOD'S WILL, I'LL CERTAINLY FIND IT!

I PRAY THAT YOU DO.

24

IN DAMASCUS, STAY OUT OF SIGHT UNTIL I SNIFF OUT THE BLASPHEMOUS RODENTS.

WE'LL TEACH THEM TO MAKE A MOCKERY OF ALL WE HOLD...

...HOLY...

I AM...

...JESUS, THE ONE YOU ARE PERSECUTING.[1]

WHY DO YOU FIGHT AGAINST ME, SAUL?

THIS IS NOT WHAT I SIGNED UP FOR.

UHHHHHHH.

WHAT... WHAT WOULD YOU HAVE ME DO, LORD?

GET UP.

GO TO THE CITY.

THERE YOU WILL LEARN WHAT YOU MUST DO.

I HAVE APPEARED TODAY TO APPOINT YOU AS A TRUE SERVANT OF GOD, TO OPEN PEOPLE'S EYES AND TURN THEM FROM DARKNESS TO LIGHT!

I ARRIVED IN DAMASCUS HARDLY THE HEROIC DEFENDER OF THE FAITH.

I STILL THINK WE SHOULD TAKE HIM TO THE AUTHORITIES --

THIS MAN JUDAS WHO OWNS THIS HOUSE. PEOPLE SAY HE CAN HELP.

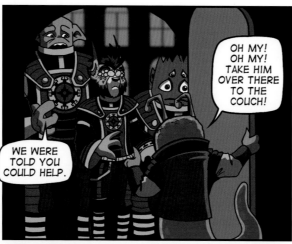

OH MY! OH MY! TAKE HIM OVER THERE TO THE COUCH!

WE WERE TOLD YOU COULD HELP.

WE'VE DONE OUR DUTY. WE'RE LEAVING.

WHAT'M I SUPPOSED TO DO WITH HIM?

NOT OUR PROBLEM.

HUNGRY, SAUL?

I AM, JUDAS.

BUT NO FOOD. THANK YOU.

NOT UNTIL GOD SPEAKS.

FATHER GOD, I BEG YOU FOR ANSWERS.

INSTEAD OF DESTROYING CHRIST FOLLOWERS, I FIND MYSELF DESTROYED BY *THE CHRIST*.

DESTROYED ONLY TO BE REBORN. YOU HAVE BEEN SPECIALLY CHOSEN BY THE LORD JESUS, TO KNOW HIS WILL, TO SEE HIS FACE, AND TO HEAR WORDS FROM HIS MOUTH. YOU WILL WITNESS TO ALL PEOPLE.

BROTHER SAUL, THE LORD JESUS WHO APPEARED TO YOU ON DAMASCUS ROAD, SENT ME HERE...

...SO THAT YOU MIGHT SEE AGAIN...

...AND BE FILLED...

...WITH THE HOLY SPIRIT.

ACTS 9:17-18

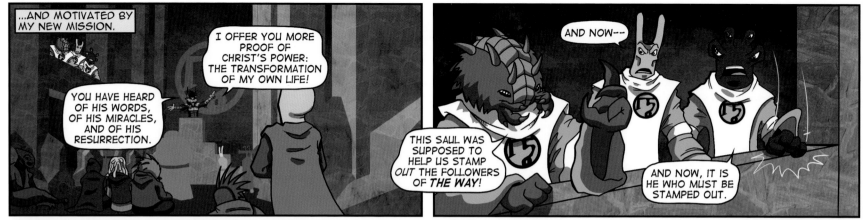

...AND MOTIVATED BY MY NEW MISSION.

I OFFER YOU MORE PROOF OF CHRIST'S POWER: THE TRANSFORMATION OF MY OWN LIFE!

YOU HAVE HEARD OF HIS WORDS, OF HIS MIRACLES, AND OF HIS RESURRECTION.

AND NOW--

THIS SAUL WAS SUPPOSED TO HELP US STAMP *OUT* THE FOLLOWERS OF *THE WAY!*

AND NOW, IT IS HE WHO MUST BE STAMPED OUT.

LET US IN!

WE MUST SPEAK TO SAUL!

THE LEADERS ARE INFURIATED BY YOUR PREACHING.

THEY ARE SEARCHING FOR YOU AS WE SPEAK.

SAUL, THEY ARE PLANNING TO KILL YOU.

IT'S TOO DANGEROUS HERE.

YOU MUST LEAVE AT ONCE, SAUL.

IN THEIR EYES, YOU ARE JUST FOLLOWERS OF YET ANOTHER FALSE PROPHET.

BUT ME, I'M ONE OF THEM WHO HAS BECOME ONE OF YOU.

OH DEAR. OH DEAR.

THE GATES ARE THE ONLY WAY OUT, BUT THEY ARE WAITING FOR YOU THERE!

THE ONLY OFFICIAL WAY OUT.

YOU MEAN TRYING TO GO UNDER THE CITY WALLS?

OR OVER THEM?

LORD, I PRAYED FOR YOU TO GIVE ME DIRECTION, PURPOSE, AND TRUTH.

THANK YOU FOR ANSWERING MY PRAYER AND FOR OPENING MY EYES TO LET ME SEE THE ANSWER.

HMMM...

BZZT

WHRR WHRR

VROOo

JERUSALEM

HOME AGAIN.

OR AM I?

ACTS 9:27

...MY LIFE! MY ZEAL! MY PASSION! ALL POINTED THE WRONG DIRECTION!

BUT THE LORD REBUKED ME!

PERHAPS WE COULD ACCEPT THAT HOW YOU WENT ABOUT YOUR CALLING WAS WRONG.

BUT YOU BECAME A CRAZY CHRIST FOLLOWER!

...WHAT WOULD *YOUR* RESPONSE BE?

OF COURSE I DID! HOW COULD I NOT?

THINK: IF JESUS REVEALED HIMSELF TO YOU AND CONFIRMED HE IS THE CHRIST AND ONE WITH GOD THE FATHER...

AND YET, LOGICALLY, WE CANNOT ACCEPT THAT PREMISE WITHOUT PROOF.

LOGICALLY, WE WOULD HAVE NO CHOICE BUT TO FOLLOW HIM.

I AM THAT PROOF! YOU ACCEPT THAT I FERVENTLY FOLLOWED GOD! YOU ACCEPT THAT I NOW JUST AS FERVENTLY FOLLOW THE CHRIST! I HAVE SEEN THE CHRIST JESUS! I HAVE HEARD HIS WORDS AND SEEN HIS LIGHT! I STILL FOLLOW THE GOD OF OUR FATHERS, BUT NOW I UNDERSTAND SO MUCH MORE!

HE PREACHES CHRIST AS FERVENTLY AS HE ONCE PERSECUTED CHRIST...

HE ENGAGES THE HELLENISTS, THE VERY PEOPLE STEPHEN MINISTERED TO.

HE HAS MUCH PRIDE.

YOU HAVE A "VISION" ON THE SIDE OF THE ROAD AND EXPECT US TO ABANDON OUR FAITH?

I EXPECT YOU TO FOLLOW YOUR FAITH TO THE LOGICAL CONCLUSION!

AND THE "LOGICAL CONCLUSION" IS ACCEPTING AS MESSIAH ONE WHO WAS PUT TO DEATH BY OUR OPPRESSORS?

THE CHRIST, OUR MESSIAH, WAS KILLED TO SAVE US FROM THE OPPRESSION OF OUR SINFUL NATURE, NOT--

SAUL!

MAY WE SPEAK TO YOU?

I WAS HAVING A CONVERSATION...

YES, WE OVERHEARD YOUR "CONVERSATION."

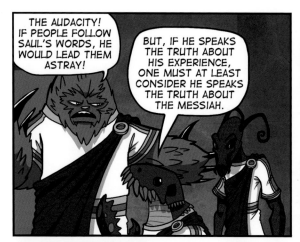

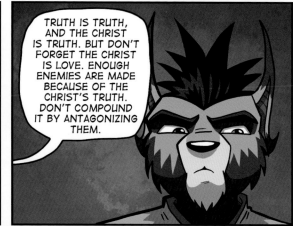

THEY TRULY BELIEVE YOU'RE A THREAT AND THEY'LL KILL YOU FOR IT.

I UNDERSTAND. I ONCE THOUGHT AS THEY DO.

WHAT NOW?

YOU GREW UP IN CILICIA, DID YOU NOT?

YES JAMES, I'M FROM TARSUS.

WHAT I'M GOING TO SUGGEST MAY BE HARD FOR YOU TO ACCEPT--

"--WE THINK MAYBE YOU SHOULD BE OUT OF THE PUBLIC EYE FOR A LITTLE WHILE."

I FLED FROM JERUSALEM, MY SOUL FILLED WITH QUESTIONS.

IS *THIS* TRULY GOD'S PLAN FOR ME?

A LIFE TURNED UPSIDE DOWN NOT SO I COULD PREACH THE GOOD NEWS OF THE RESURRECTED CHRIST...

...BUT SO I COULD GO INTO HIDING?

WELCOME HOME, MY FRIEND!

ACTS 9:30

IT'S BEEN A WHILE!

GUESS WHAT? I FOLLOW *THE WAY*, JUST LIKE YOU! THERE'S A GROUP OF US HERE.

I CAN'T WAIT TO HEAR YOUR STORY, OLD FRIEND!

BUT FIRST... I NEED A PLACE TO STAY... AND A JOB.

I'D LOVE FOR YOU TO STAY WITH ME...

AND I YOURS.

"...AND HELP WITH MY TENT BUSINESS."

WELCOME SAUL INTO OUR LITTLE COMMUNITY.

SAUL WAS IN SOME TROUBLE IN JERUSALEM.

TO SAUL, FROM BARNABAS.

I HEAR YOU ARE A GOOD FIT WITH THE BELIEVERS THERE OVER THE LAST YEAR!

SAUL, BE ENCOURAGED! I AM IN ANTIOCH, A PLACE FILLED WITH GENTILES LONGING FOR OUR MESSAGE, ALTHOUGH THEY DO NOT UNDERSTAND WHY--

I SHOULD BE OUT THERE, DOING SOMETHING! NOT HERE, WAITING--

--I SHOULD BE WHERE THE ACTION IS!

INSTEAD OF MOANING ABOUT BEING HERE, MAYBE YOU SHOULD FIND OUT WHY YOU'RE HERE.

SAUL, HOW LONG WAS MOSES A SHEPHERD BEFORE HE LED OUR PEOPLE OUT OF EGYPT?

WHY?

WHY, LORD? I AM UNIQUE AMONG MEN, AS A JEW AND A ROMAN, LEARNED IN THINGS OF THE JEWS AND THE GENTILES! WHY AM I HERE, INSTEAD OF BEING USED BY YOU?

...I CANNOT EXPLAIN IT.

IT WAS THE CHRIST. HE SHOWED ME SUCH... BEAUTY. AND... AND HOLINESS.

HEAVEN!

SOMETHING I DID NOT DESERVE TO SEE. NO ONE DESERVES TO SEE WHAT I SAW.

AND I THINK THAT'S THE POINT.

I HAD SO MUCH TO BOAST ABOUT BEFORE.

NOW?

NOTHING, EXCEPT THE BOAST ALL OF US CAN MAKE.

CHRIST LOVES ME.

AFTER THAT, I DID NOT QUESTION WHERE I WAS. I DID WHAT I KNEW I WAS SUPPOSED TO DO.

...AND HE LOVES YOU TOO!

HE SET ME FREE! HE'LL SET YOU FREE!

BUT THE SHACKLES THE CHRIST FREES US FROM AREN'T WHAT WE EXPECTED...

ON THE STREET...

...AT WORK...

...HOPE YOUR TENT KEEPS YOU WARM AND DRY.

I AM.

WELL, YOU SEE...

YOU'RE SAUL, AREN'T YOU? THE CHRIST-FOLLOWER?

WHY ARE OUR LEADERS SO THREATENED BY A DEAD CULT LEADER?

...AND IN THE FACE OF ADVERSITY...

--MAY WE SPEAK WITH YOU?

WE'VE HEARD THE LIES YOU'VE BEEN PREACHING AND IT MUST STOP.

YOU DON'T LOOK LIKE YOU'RE LOOKING FOR TENTS.

IMMEDIATELY. OR THERE WILL BE CONSEQUENCES...

I AM A TARGET, AND PUT YOU ALL IN DANGER.

WE DO NOT CARE! YOU MUST NOT WORRY ABOUT US!

THE CHRIST HIMSELF WARNED US OF THIS!

I HEARD YOU WERE ORDERED TO STOP PREACHING OR RISK PUNISHMENT! WHY WOULD YOU CONTINUE?

BECAUSE THEY CALL IT HERESY, BUT IN TRUTH, IT IS "GOOD NEWS", FOR ME AND FOR YOU! LET ME TELL YOU MORE...

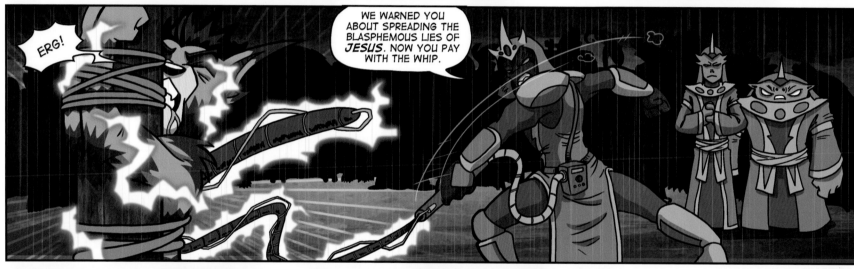

ERG!

WE WARNED YOU ABOUT SPREADING THE BLASPHEMOUS LIES OF *JESUS*. NOW YOU PAY WITH THE WHIP.

...FLOGGED, AND STILL YOU TELL PEOPLE ABOUT YOUR CHRIST?

NO SURPRISE, I GUESS, IF WHAT YOU SAY IS TRUE, YOU WOULD RISK FLOGGING.

IT IS TRUE, AND I RISK THE PUNISHMENT SO I CAN SHARE THAT TRUTH WITH PEOPLE LIKE YOU!

AGAIN YOU DEFY US! BY LAW YOU MUST STOP.

IT... WON'T HAPPEN...

...WE ARE ALL THE SAME, JEW AND GENTILE.

WE ALL DESERVE JUDGMENT FOR OUR SIN. AND WE ALL--

SAUL, SOMEONE IS HERE TO SEE YOU.

SAUL, HOW ARE YOU OLD FRIEND?

BARNABAS!!! I AM DOING WELL, ESPECIALLY NOW THAT YOU'RE HERE.

I HEAR THAT YOU PREACH IN THE FACE OF BRUTAL PERSECUTION.

WHAT IS MY SUFFERING COMPARED TO MY LORD'S?

NOW, IT'S TIME FOR YOU TO LEAVE. I NEED YOU SAUL. ANTIOCH NEEDS YOU.

I AM NOTHING SPECIAL. IF THERE'S ONE THING I'VE LEARNED HERE, IT'S THAT.

LET ME EXPLAIN.

THE NEW BELIEVERS IN ANTIOCH WANT TO KNOW CHRIST, BUT THEIR GODS ALLOW EVIL.

ENCOURAGE IT, EVEN!

OUR MISSION IN ANTIOCH HAS BEEN SUCCESSFUL, BUT WE NEED YOUR HELP!

PAUL, YOU HAVE A PASSIONATE UNDERSTANDING OF GOD AND HIS WAYS.

PLUS, YOU UNDERSTAND HOW THE GENTILES THINK!

I'VE DONE A LOT HERE, AND--

YOU HAVE. YOU TURNED WHAT YOU THOUGHT TO BE EXILE INTO A MINISTRY.

I JUST DON'T KNOW WHAT TO SAY.

I DO.

SAY "YES," SAUL!

YOU DID AMAZING WORK HERE! I THINK THOSE OF US YOU'LL BE LEAVING BEHIND WILL BE MORE THAN CAPABLE TO CONTINUE IT!

OKAY...

ACTS 11:25-26

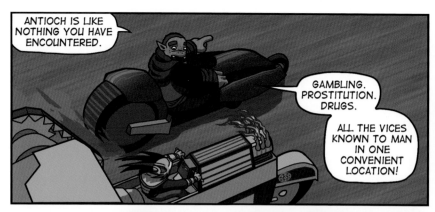

ANTIOCH IS LIKE NOTHING YOU HAVE ENCOUNTERED.

GAMBLING. PROSTITUTION. DRUGS.

ALL THE VICES KNOWN TO MAN IN ONE CONVENIENT LOCATION!

PEOPLE HERE ARE OPEN TO OUR MESSAGE! BUT LIKE CHRIST'S PARABLE OF THE SEEDS, IT IS DIFFICULT FOR SEEDS TO GROW AMONG WEEDS.

SOME OF THE FIRST SEEDS OF CHRIST'S MESSAGE CAME HERE BECAUSE OF STEPHEN'S DEATH. AND YOUR PERSECUTION IN JERUSALEM.

SOME MAY STILL REMEMBER--

YOU!!!

HOW DARE YOU SHOW YOUR FACE HERE!?!

HOLD, FRIEND...

I... I...

WHAT YOU DID TO US...WE CANNOT EVEN SPEAK YOUR NAME! WE MUST SPIT IT--

SAUL!

PTOOO

UGH.

I...I'M SORRY...

HAVE YOU NOT HEARD? SAUL HAS CHANGED! HE BECAME ONE OF US YEARS AGO!

I TRUST YOU, BARNABAS.

BUT I CANNOT TRUST HIM!

NOT AFTER WHAT HE DID!

I WORKED IN ANTIOCH FOR A TIME, UNTIL SOME PROPHETS FROM JERUSALEM ARRIVED.

THE MESSAGE WE BRING IS DIRE.

THROUGH THE HOLY SPIRIT I'VE FORESEEN A GREAT FAMINE!

THIS FAMINE WILL BRING EVEN MORE HARDSHIP, BUT THEY DO NOT FEEL THEY CAN LEAVE THEIR MINISTRY THERE!

WE MUST SEND RELIEF TO OUR BROTHERS AND SISTERS IN JUDEA. AND I WANT TO TAKE IT TO THEM.

THE PEOPLE OF THE CHURCH IN JUDEA ARE ALREADY SCATTERED FROM THEIR HOMES.

WE HAVE HEARD AGABUS' PROPHECY.

I AM ONE WHO IS WILLING AND ABLE TO ADMIT WHEN I AM WRONG.

AND ABOUT SAUL, I WAS WRONG.

YOU CAN SAY THAT AGAIN!

ONCE IS ENOUGH, I THINK.

SAUL HAS BEEN A GREAT HELP TO US HERE IN ANTIOCH.

AND WHILE IT WOULD PAIN ME FOR HIM TO LEAVE, I THINK IT WOULD BE APPROPRIATE IF OUR HELP WAS DELIVERED BY SAUL'S HAND.

SO I RETURNED TO JERUSALEM TO HELP THOSE I ONCE PERSECUTED.

BARNABAS! SAUL! MANY, MANY THANKS TO YOU!

PRAISE BE TO GOD!!!

CHAPTER TWO:
A HOLY MISSION

THE LORD RESCUES THE GODLY;

HE IS THEIR FORTRESS IN TIMES OF TROUBLE.

THE LORD HELPS THEM,

RESCUING THEM FROM THE WICKED.

HE SAVES THEM,

AND THEY FIND SHELTER IN HIM.

-PSALM 37:39-40 (NLT)

SAUL, MEET MY COUSIN, JOHN MARK! HE'S COMING WITH US BACK TO ANTIOCH.

AN HONOR, SIR, TO MEET YOU.

THE HONOR IS MINE!

WE CAN ALWAYS USE HELP!

OH, I'LL DO WHATEVER I CAN!

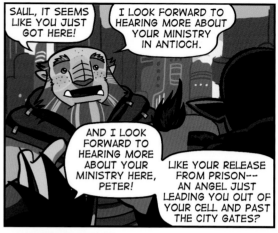

SAUL, IT SEEMS LIKE YOU JUST GOT HERE!

I LOOK FORWARD TO HEARING MORE ABOUT YOUR MINISTRY IN ANTIOCH.

AND I LOOK FORWARD TO HEARING MORE ABOUT YOUR MINISTRY HERE, PETER!

LIKE YOUR RELEASE FROM PRISON-- AN ANGEL JUST LEADING YOU OUT OF YOUR CELL AND PAST THE CITY GATES?

THE LORD IS MOVING.

THAT HE IS!

AND WE MUST FOLLOW.

THAT WE WILL!

SO WE RETURNED FROM JERUSALEM TO BE WITH OUR MINISTRY AND OUR FRIENDS.

BUT THE LORD HAD OTHER PLANS FOR US...

WELCOME BACK!

BROTHERS IN CHRIST, LET US WORSHIP GOD, FAST, AND PRAY TOGETHER.

LORD JESUS, THROUGH YOUR HOLY SPIRIT MAY YOU GUIDE BARNABAS AND SAUL TOWARDS RIGHTEOUSNESS.

ACTS 12:25, ACTS 13:1-3

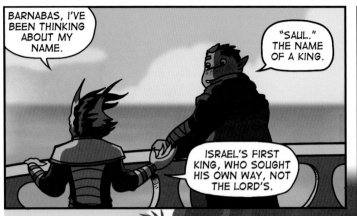

BARNABAS, I'VE BEEN THINKING ABOUT MY NAME.

"SAUL." THE NAME OF A KING.

ISRAEL'S FIRST KING, WHO SOUGHT HIS OWN WAY, NOT THE LORD'S.

I HAVE ANOTHER NAME. A ROMAN NAME.

"PAUL."

IT MEANS SMALL. OR LITTLE. OR HUMBLE.

HMM.

ALL DESCRIBE YOU, MY FRIEND!

PAUL IT IS!

IN THOSE EARLY DAYS, ARRIVING IN THOSE NEW PLACES, OUR FIRST DESTINATION WAS ALWAYS THE LOCAL JEWISH SYNAGOGUE.

WHAT BETTER PLACE TO BRING THE MESSAGE OF THE CHRIST THAN TO THE PEOPLE WHO ALREADY KNEW AND UNDERSTOOD HALF THE MESSAGE?

--THE CHRIST DID NOT PREACH AGAINST THE LAW OF MOSES, BUT HIS DEATH FULFILLED IT.

A PURE SACRIFICE, THE ONLY PERFECT SACRIFICE THAT COULD BE MADE FOR OUR SINS.

WHY WOULD WE FOLLOW YOUR GOD INSTEAD OF OURS? ALREADY, ON THIS ISLE OF GREEKS, WE REFUSE *THEIR* GODS!

BECAUSE THE GOD OF ABRAHAM, MOSES, AND DAVID IS THE GOD OF JESUS...

WE BROUGHT THE MESSAGE FROM CITY TO CITY.

...SYNAGOGUE TO SYNAGOGUE.

--AND LIFE CAN BE FOUND IN *HIM*. LIFE MORE ABUNDANT!

YOU, SIR. THE GOVERNOR DEMANDS YOUR PRESENCE.

THIS SHOULD BE INTERESTING.

AHHH! SO YOU ARE THE ONES WHO BRING A NEW MESSAGE TO THE JEWS HERE!

BAH! THEY SAY THEY ARE JEWS, BUT THEY COME WITH A PERVERTED MESSAGE!

THIS IS ELYMAS BAR-JESUS. HE IS A POWERFUL PROPHET AND SORCERER-- AND JEW.

SINCE YOU, TOO, ARE JEWISH, I'M INTERESTED IN YOUR WAYS.

I HAVE SHOWN THE LORD GOVERNOR SIGNS AND WONDERS FOR HIS EYES!

I HAVE SPOKEN WISDOM AND PROPHECY FOR HIS EARS!

AND I HAVE GIVEN HIM POWER FOR HIS HEART!

ENOUGH! YOU CHILD OF THE DEVIL! IT IS *YOU* WHO PERVERTS THE MESSAGE OF OUR *LORD*!!!

YOU'VE CLOUDED THE EYES OF THESE PEOPLE WITH YOUR FALSE PROPHECIES! BUT NO MORE!

FOR BEHOLD, THE HAND OF THE *LORD* IS ON *YOU*, IN TRUTH THIS TIME!

ELYMAS?

WHAT... WHAT ARE YOU...

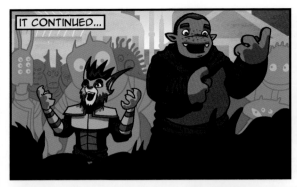

IT CONTINUED...

...THE MISSION...

...THE PREACHING...

...THE JOURNEY.

SO NOW, NORTH. WE WILL TAKE THE LORD'S MESSAGE WHERE FEW-- IF ANY!-- HAVE HEARD IT.

WE'VE GONE SO FAR ALREADY...

AND THEN, ANOTHER CHANGE.

I THINK WE'LL HEAD TO PERGA, FIRST. THEY HAVE AN ACTIVE SYNAGOGUE THERE.

JOHN MARK, ARE YOU COMING?

COUSIN, COME NOW, THIS IS NO JOKING MATTER.

I'M TIRED.

AND YOU WILL TAKE ME EVEN FURTHER AWAY?

I... I CANNOT.

I HAVE BEEN AWAY FROM HOME TOO LONG...

SHUNK

COME, BARNABAS.

HE MADE HIS CHOICE, DISAPPOINTING THOUGH IT MAY BE, AND SO HAVE WE.

WE HAVE WORK TO DO.

--THUS SAYS THE WORD OF THE LORD.

NOW, WE WELCOME OUR BROTHERS FROM JERUSALEM!

AND WE ASK YOU, DO YOU HAVE ANY WORDS OF ENCOURAGEMENT OR NEWS FROM JERUSALEM TO SHARE WITH US?

AS A MATTER OF FACT, WE DO. WE BRING *GOOD NEWS*!

FELLOW KINSMEN, MEN OF ISRAEL, AND YOU GENTILES WHO WORSHIP GOD!

LEND AUDIENCE TO WHAT I HAVE TO SAY.

THE GOD OF ISRAEL CHOSE OUR FATHERS.

HE BROUGHT THEM OUT OF EGYPT, GAVE THEM CANAAN, LED THEM WITH THE JUDGES, THEN GAVE THEM KING SAUL.

AFTER REMOVING SAUL, HE MADE DAVID THEIR KING.

AND I WANT TO TELL YOU ABOUT WHAT GOD PROMISED REGARDING DAVID'S LINEAGE.

A *SAVIOR*.

ISRAEL'S SAVIOR.

FROM THE LINE OF DAVID.

JESUS.

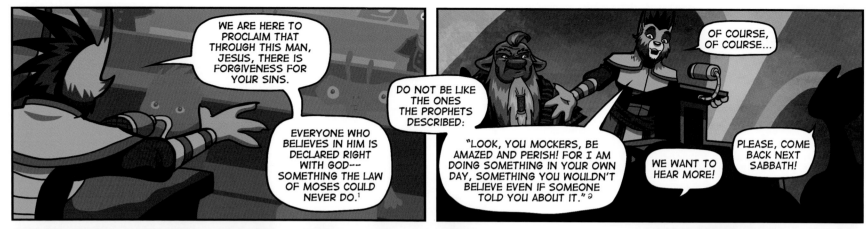

WE ARE HERE TO PROCLAIM THAT THROUGH THIS MAN, JESUS, THERE IS FORGIVENESS FOR YOUR SINS.

EVERYONE WHO BELIEVES IN HIM IS DECLARED RIGHT WITH GOD-- SOMETHING THE LAW OF MOSES COULD NEVER DO.[1]

DO NOT BE LIKE THE ONES THE PROPHETS DESCRIBED:

"LOOK, YOU MOCKERS, BE AMAZED AND PERISH! FOR I AM DOING SOMETHING IN YOUR OWN DAY, SOMETHING YOU WOULDN'T BELIEVE EVEN IF SOMEONE TOLD YOU ABOUT IT."[2]

OF COURSE, OF COURSE...

WE WANT TO HEAR MORE!

PLEASE, COME BACK NEXT SABBATH!

THE FOLLOWING SABBATH

--AND THE CHRIST IS, THEN, THE PERFECT FULFILLMENT OF THE LAW OF MOSES.

NO! YOUR CHRIST, HE CANNOT REPLACE MOSES' LAW!

HOW DARE YOU?

I WAS ASKED TO COME!

AND THIS CROWD WOULD INDICATE THAT PEOPLE ARE INTERESTED IN THIS MESSAGE!

THE GENTILE CONVERTS ASKED YOU TO COME!

THEY WERE NOT BORN INTO THE PROMISE.

YOU ACT AS IF GOD'S SALVATION MIGHT BE FOR ANYONE WHO ASKS!

YOU FINALLY GOT SOMETHING RIGHT.

WE CAME TO YOU FIRST WITH THE WORD OF GOD.

YOU REJECT IT, SO WE WILL TURN TO THE GENTILES.

FOR GOD HAS COMMANDED US, SAYING: "I HAVE MADE YOU A LIGHT TO THE GENTILES, TO BRING SALVATION TO THE FARTHEST CORNERS OF THE EARTH."[3]

AND SUCH WAS OUR JOURNEY.

FROM CITY TO CITY, BOLDLY BRINGING CHRIST'S MESSAGE FIRST INTO THE SYNAGOGUE, THEN TO THE GENTILES.

UNTIL FORCED TO LEAVE BY THOSE JEWISH LEADERS WHO SAW *THE WAY* AS A PERVERSION OF THEIR LAW, NOT THE FULFILLMENT.

BUT IN SPITE OF PERSECUTION, MANY BELIEVED AND THE NUMBER OF THOSE WHO FOLLOWED *THE WAY* GREW.

ACTS 13:38-49, [1]ACTS 13:38-39 (NLT) [2]ACTS 13:41 (NLT), [3]ACTS 13:47 (NLT)

THE CITY OF LYSTRA.

BUT WE ARE *GENTILES*!

WHEN THE CHRIST WAS HERE, HE TAUGHT AND HEALED WITH POWER, NOT JUST FOR THE JEWISH PEOPLE.

BUT FOR ANYONE WHO HAD FAITH.

THE MESSAGE OF THE CHRIST IS FOR ALL PEOPLE. YOU. ME. EVERYONE.

HEY, YEAH! I BELIEVE!

I'VE BEEN LAME SINCE I WAS BORN. NEVER BEEN ABLE TO WALK.

BUT I'VE HEARD YOU SPEAKING. I'VE BEEN WATCHING YOU.

WHAT YOU SAY. IT'S REAL.

YES. IT IS.

YOU BELIEVE.

YOU HAVE FAITH IN THE CHRIST.

STAND UP, YOU. GET UP ON YOUR FEET.

WHAT'S GOING ON?

I CAN WALK! I CAN REALLY WALK!

I DON'T BELIEVE IT!

I'VE SEEN HIM EVERY DAY SINCE WE WERE CHILDREN, BEGGIN', AND NOW...

THE GODS! THE GODS HAVE COME AND TAKEN ON FLESHLY FORM!

ACTS 14:12-19

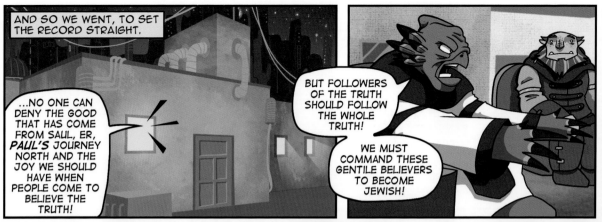

AND SO WE WENT, TO SET THE RECORD STRAIGHT.

...NO ONE CAN DENY THE GOOD THAT HAS COME FROM SAUL, ER, *PAUL'S* JOURNEY NORTH AND THE JOY WE SHOULD HAVE WHEN PEOPLE COME TO BELIEVE THE TRUTH!

BUT FOLLOWERS OF THE TRUTH SHOULD FOLLOW THE WHOLE TRUTH!

WE MUST COMMAND THESE GENTILE BELIEVERS TO BECOME JEWISH!

PLEASE LISTEN, EVERYONE!

YOU ARE AWARE THAT GOD CHOSE ME TO PREACH TO THE GENTILES SO THEY MIGHT HEAR THE GOSPEL AND BELIEVE.

AND GUESS WHAT? TURNS OUT, THE HOLY SPIRIT ACTUALLY TOUCHED THEIR HEARTS!

JUST LIKE HE TOUCHED OURS!

THERE'S NO DIFFERENCE BETWEEN THEM AND US!

OUR HEARTS ARE PURIFIED BY FAITH!

YES, BUT THERE IS STILL THE *LAW!*

THE LAW!!!

LET'S FACE THE FACTS! NONE OF US-- AND NONE OF OUR ANCESTORS-- CAN KEEP THE WHOLE LAW!

WE'RE ALL SINNERS!

BUT THROUGH GRACE-- THE GRACE OF THE LORD JESUS CHRIST-- WE'RE ALL SAVED!

DO YOU *REALLY* WANT TO PUT THESE *NEW* CONVERTS UNDER THE *OLD* LAW?

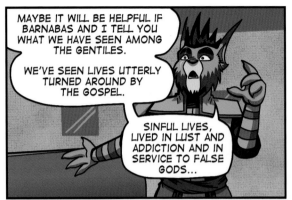

MAYBE IT WILL BE HELPFUL IF BARNABAS AND I TELL YOU WHAT WE HAVE SEEN AMONG THE GENTILES.

WE'VE SEEN LIVES UTTERLY TURNED AROUND BY THE GOSPEL.

SINFUL LIVES, LIVED IN LUST AND ADDICTION AND IN SERVICE TO FALSE GODS...

ALL WITHOUT BECOMING JEWISH.

...NOW LIVED IN SERVICE TO *CHRIST JESUS!*

MIRACLES ARE HAPPENING AND PRAYERS ARE BEING ANSWERED.

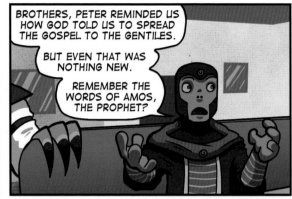

BROTHERS, PETER REMINDED US HOW GOD TOLD US TO SPREAD THE GOSPEL TO THE GENTILES.

BUT EVEN THAT WAS NOTHING NEW.

REMEMBER THE WORDS OF AMOS, THE PROPHET?

IF NOT PETER, THEY MUST LISTEN TO JAMES.

GOD SPOKE THROUGH HIM, SAYING, "AFTER THIS I WILL RETURN AND BUILD AGAIN DAVID'S FALLEN TABERNACLE, THAT EVEN ALL THE GENTILES MAY SEEK AFTER ME."

LET'S NOT MAKE IT DIFFICULT AMONG THE GENTILES WHO TURN TO GOD!

WE'RE SEEING A TRANSFORMATION OF THE HEART IN THE GENTILES, REVEALED IN A LIFE LIVED FOR CHRIST.

WE WILL ASK THEM TO ABSTAIN FROM SINFUL BEHAVIORS LIKE SEXUAL IMMORALITY AND INDULGING IN FOOD OFFERED TO IDOLS, STRANGLED ANIMALS, AND BLOOD.

WE PUT IT IN WRITING.

WELL, PAUL. BARNABAS. THIS IS THE LETTER WE HAVE WRITTEN FOR THE GENTILE BELIEVERS.

THAT IS WHY YOU WON'T BE BRINGING THIS LETTER ALONE...

PEOPLE ARE GOING TO BE SUSPECT IF WE BRING THAT LETTER, SINCE IT ESSENTIALLY EXPRESSES OUR OPINION.

"...JUDAS AND I WILL BE COMING WITH YOU, TO GIVE ADDED CREDIBILITY."

WE TOOK THE DECLARATION TO THE NEW GENTILE BELIEVERS AND THE JEWISH BELIEVERS.

PAUL, I CAN'T TELL YOU ENOUGH HOW RELIEVED I AM ABOUT THE COUNCIL'S DECISION.

I CAN IMAGINE.

THE LETTER FROM JAMES IS A HUGE HELP.

LET'S TAKE IT TO THE CHURCHES AROUND GALATIA.

I LOVE THAT IDEA.

PAUL, I'D LIKE TO BRING JOHN MARK WITH US AGAIN.

GIVE HIM A CHANCE TO SEE WHAT HE MISSED LAST TIME.

BARNABAS, HAVE YOU LOST YOUR MIND?

WE NEEDED HIM AND HE ABANDONED US!

PAUL, YOU OF ALL PEOPLE UNDERSTAND HOW INDIVIDUALS CAN CHANGE.

THAT WAS YEARS AGO. MY NEPHEW--

BEING YOUR COUSIN DOES NOT GIVE HIM A PASS.

I'M AMAZED AT YOU, PAUL. I DEFENDED YOU IN A SIMILAR ARGUMENT.

I WILL NOT TRAVEL WITH HIM.

THEN YOU WILL NOT TRAVEL WITH ME.

WE'LL COVER MORE GROUND THAT WAY.

RIGHT?

NOW WHAT, PAUL? YOU'RE JUST SPLITTING UP?

I NEED SOMEONE TO COME WITH ME, SILAS. SOMEONE TO TAKE BARNABAS' PLACE.

LET'S TALK TO THE ELDERS.

I HAVE AN IDEA...

AND SO BARNABAS AND JOHN MARK HEADED TO CYPRUS...

...WHILE I WENT TO SYRIA AND CILICIA, THEN TO DERBE AND LYSTRA.

I BEGAN MY SECOND MISSIONARY JOURNEY.

PAUL! WELCOME BACK!

HI PAUL!

THANK YOU!

MY NEW COMPANION: SILAS HIMSELF.

IS THAT TIMOTHY I SEE? YOU'VE GROWN UP.

IT IS GOOD TO SEE YOU, SIR.

I'VE COME TO VISIT THE CHURCH HERE. AND I'M DELIVERING A LETTER FROM THE ELDERS IN JERUSALEM ABOUT BEHAVIOR NEW BELIEVERS SHOULD FOLLOW.

LIKE THE "BECOMING JEWISH" DECISION?

EXACTLY.

THAT'S A CONTROVERSIAL DECISION AROUND HERE.

AS YOU KNOW, MY HUSBAND IS GREEK.

YES, I REMEMBER.

AND I HAVE NEVER OFFICIALLY BECOME JEWISH.

SILAS AND I CAME TO ENCOURAGE THE FOLLOWERS HERE, BUT I HAVE BEEN ENCOURAGED MYSELF, SEEING HOW WELL THEY ARE DOING.

JESUS MADE IT EASY WHEN HE SAID WHAT THE MOST IMPORTANT COMMANDMENTS WERE.

"LOVE THE LORD YOUR GOD WITH ALL YOUR HEART" AND "LOVE YOUR NEIGHBOR AS YOURSELF"!

YOU'RE EXACTLY RIGHT MY YOUNG FRIEND!

CAN I GET YOU ANYTHING?

HE IS VERY WISE FOR ONE SO YOUNG.

AND VERY ENTHUSIASTIC.

HE WANTS TO BE JUST LIKE YOU.

SPREADING THE GOSPEL TO UNBELIEVERS AROUND THE WORLD.

BEING HIS MOTHER, I DO NOT WANT HIM TO LEAVE.

BUT I ALSO WANT HIM TO FOLLOW THE LORD'S WILL.

WE COULD USE HELP ON THIS TRIP.

IF YOU WOULD BE OPEN TO IT.

MIND IF I JOIN YOU?

OH, YES SIR. SURE.

YOUR GRANDMOTHER SURE CAN COOK. I HAVEN'T EATEN LIKE THAT FOR A LONG TIME.

TRUST ME, SHE DOESN'T COOK LIKE THAT EVERY DAY.

THIS WAS A SPECIAL OCCASION.

THAT IT IS.

YOUR MOTHER TELLS ME YOU WANT TO TAKE PART IN THE MINISTRY.

YESSIR. I'D LIKE NOTHING MORE. I FEEL A CALLING, I GUESS YOU'D SAY.

TIMOTHY, I'D LIKE YOU TO JOIN US ON OUR CURRENT MISSION.

YOU MEAN IT? YOU TRULY MEAN IT, SIR?

BUT I'M SO YOUNG.

YOU ARE ALSO EAGER AND YOU ARE "CALLED." THERE'S JUST ONE THING. YOU'RE ALSO HALF GREEK. AND IF YOU PLAN TO MINISTER WITH ME TO THE GENTILES, THERE'S NO PROBLEM--

--BUT IF YOU PLAN TO MINISTER TO THE JEWS--

--YOU MUST BECOME A JEW.

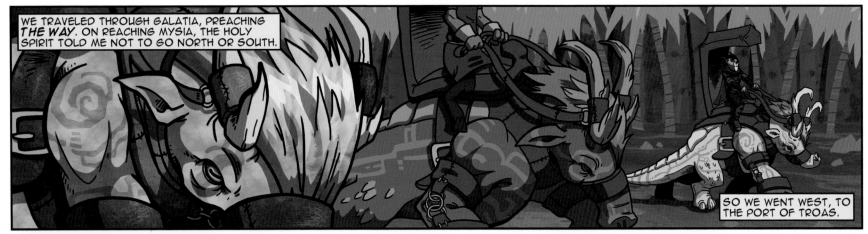

WE TRAVELED THROUGH GALATIA, PREACHING *THE WAY*. ON REACHING MYSIA, THE HOLY SPIRIT TOLD ME NOT TO GO NORTH OR SOUTH.

SO WE WENT WEST, TO THE PORT OF TROAS.

WHERE TO NOW, PAUL?

GOOD QUESTION, SILAS.

THERE ARE SO MANY PLACES THAT WE MISSED BECAUSE WE FELT LED HERE.

THERE MUST BE A PURPOSE!

IN THE MORNING, WE CAN SEE IF THERE ARE BELIEVERS HERE.

RIGHT.

I'VE HEARD THAT DOCTOR AND WRITER, THE ONE WHO'S BEEN INTERVIEWING PEOPLE ABOUT THE CHRIST JESUS, IS AROUND HERE.

HEEELP USSSS!

WHO'S THERE!

AND LEAVING TROAS, WE HEADED TO PHILIPPI, THE CHIEF ROMAN COLONY IN MACEDONIA. NOT WHERE I EXPECTED TO END UP WHEN I STARTED, BUT LITTLE IN MY LIFE ENDED UP AS I EXPECTED.

WE'RE HERE. WHAT NOW?

WE FIND THE "MAN FROM MACEDONIA" FROM MY DREAM.

AND THEN WE HELP THIS "MAN FROM MACEDONIA"?

BUT WHERE? THERE AREN'T ENOUGH JEWS IN PHILIPPI TO WARRANT A SYNAGOGUE.

NO. BUT THE JEWS HERE WOULD FIND A PLACE TO PRAY ON THE SABBATH, WITH OR WITHOUT A SYNAGOGUE.

LOOK, THERE...

GREETINGS, BROTHERS AND SISTERS!

GREETINGS! YOU, GENTLEMEN, YOU ARE JEWISH, NO? LIKE US?

YOU ARE WELCOME TO PRAY WITH US!

I AM LYDIA.

PAUL. MY NAME IS PAUL.

I'M SORRY, I WAS TOLD TO COME HERE... BUT I WAS NOT TOLD WHAT TO EXPECT.

"TOLD" TO COME?

YES. GOD GAVE ME A VISION.

PERHAPS YOU WERE SENT TO TEACH US? AS YOU CAN SEE, WE HAVE NO SYNAGOGUE. AND WE HAVE LITTLE OPPORTUNITY TO LEARN MORE ABOUT THE GOD WE WORSHIP.

I WOULD BE HONORED TO TEACH YOU.

ALTHOUGH SOME OF WHAT I TEACH MAY NOT BE WHAT YOU EXPECT...

LOOKS LIKE PAUL'S "MAN OF MACEDONIA" TURNED OUT TO BE A WOMAN!

I'D LIKE TO HEAR MORE. AND MY HUSBAND SHOULD HEAR THIS! AND MY KIDS...

SHALL WE MEET BACK HERE? TOMORROW?

YES. YES, THANK YOU...

THE NEXT DAY...

AH, LYDIA!

AS PROMISED! PLEASE TELL MY FAMILY, PAUL! TELL THEM WHAT YOU TOLD ME!

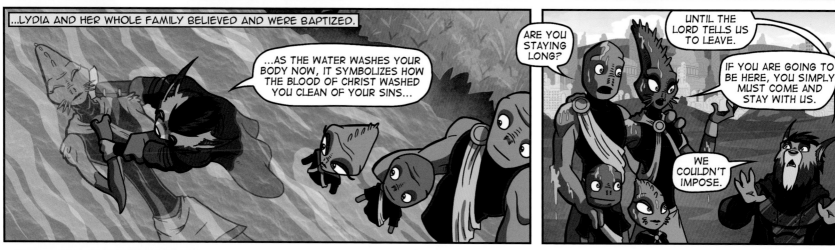

...LYDIA AND HER WHOLE FAMILY BELIEVED AND WERE BAPTIZED.

...AS THE WATER WASHES YOUR BODY NOW, IT SYMBOLIZES HOW THE BLOOD OF CHRIST WASHED YOU CLEAN OF YOUR SINS...

ARE YOU STAYING LONG?

UNTIL THE LORD TELLS US TO LEAVE.

IF YOU ARE GOING TO BE HERE, YOU SIMPLY MUST COME AND STAY WITH US.

WE COULDN'T IMPOSE.

IT'S NO IMPOSITION. WE INSIST!

NO, WE—

THERE'S NO POINT IN ARGUING WITH HER. YOU WON'T WIN.

THE NEXT DAY...

PAUL, LET ME THANK YOU AGAIN.

FOR WHAT?

FOR NOT ARGUING WITH LYDIA. THEIR BEDS ARE MOST COMFORTABLE!

WHERE DO PEOPLE MEET IN THIS CITY?

LOOKING TO CRASH SOME CONVERSATIONS, HM?

THAT'S USUALLY THE BEST WAY TO GET PEOPLE TO LISTEN TO US...

ACTS 16:11-15

AHHHH! IT'S THEM! SERVANTS OF THE MOST HIGH GOD!

THEY'LL SHOW YOU SALVATION!

I KNOW!

SALVATION! SALVATION! YOU'LL SEE!

SOMEHOW I DON'T THINK PEOPLE ARE GOING TO LISTEN TO US WITH SOMEONE LIKE HER ACTING AS OUR SPOKESPERSON...

FRIENDS OF MINE WANT TO MEET YOU. THEY WERE INTERESTED IN HEARING ABOUT MY BAPTISM, BUT I HAD A HARD TIME EXPLAINING WHY...

LISTEN TO THESE MEN!

HER AGAIN? THIS IS THE FIFTH TIME!

NO ONE TAKES US SERIOUSLY, WITH HER VOUCHING FOR OUR "SALVATION" MESSAGE.

SERVANTS OF THE MOST HIGH! THEY CAN SHOW YOU SALVATION! I KNOW! I KNOW ALL!

WHO IS SHE?

A SOOTHSAYER. A PROPHETESS.

SHE BELONGS TO A COUPLE MEN IN THE CITY WHO HAVE CREATED QUITE A BUSINESS SELLING HER WORDS.

SHE HAS SUPERNATURAL KNOWLEDGE.

HAD.

SHE *HAD* SUPERNATURAL KNOWLEDGE.

NOTHIN' LIKE A BIT OF ELECTRICITY BEFORE BED!

SECURE THEM FIRMLY. THE MAGISTRATES WILL HAVE MY HEAD IF ANYTHING HAPPENS TO THESE TWO..

WELL, CAN'T SAY I EXPECTED THIS WHEN I WAS PREPARING TO TRAVEL WITH YOU.

I'M JUST GLAD TIMOTHY ISN'T HERE.

PETER WOULD HAVE AN ANGEL RESCUE HIM BY NOW!

WHAT'S THE SONG ABOUT ANGELS?

WHEN YOU MAKE THE LORD YOUR ♫♪ --AH-- DWELLING PLACE-- ♫♪

--NO HARM WILL OVERTAKE YOU! ♫♪♪ HE'LL COMMAND ANGELS TO GUARD YOUR WAYS YOU'LL TRAMPLE LION AND SNAKE, TOO! ♫♪♪

♫♪ "BECAUSE YOU LOVE ME," SAYS THE LORD, "I WILL RESCUE YOU!" ♫♪

AW, SHUT UP!

NAW, YOU SHUT UP! IT'S NICE!

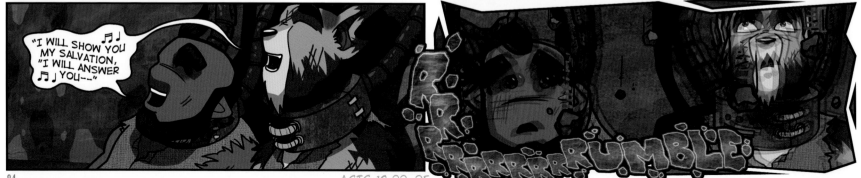

♫♪ "I WILL SHOW YOU MY SALVATION, "I WILL ANSWER ♫♪ YOU--"

RRRRRRRRUMBLE

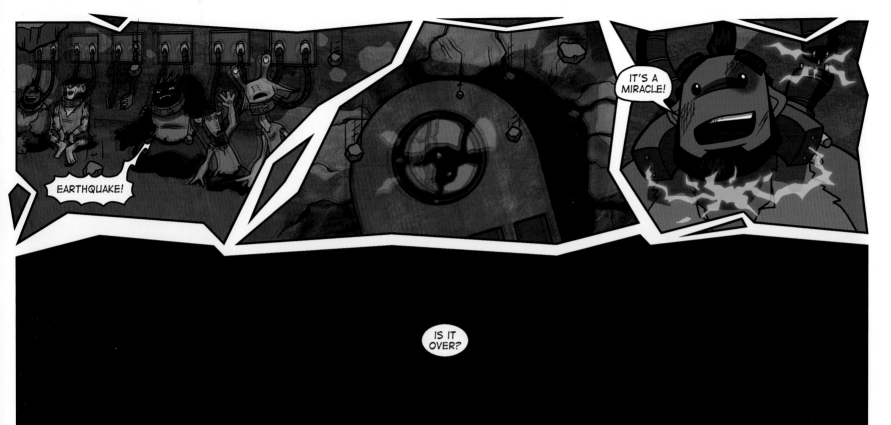

I REALLY APPRECIATE YOU TWO NOT RUNNING.

AND FOR SAVING ME FROM HURTING MYSELF.

AS FOR YOU-- PLEASE LET ME WASH YOUR WOUNDS TO SAY SORRY...

NOW, YOU SAID I WASN'T READY FOR ETERNITY. I KNOW I'M NOT.

HOW CAN A MAN LIKE ME BE SAVED?

IT IS SIMPLE. PROCLAIM THAT JESUS IS LORD AND BELIEVE IN YOUR HEART THAT GOD RAISED HIM FROM THE DEAD.

GOD WILL WASH AWAY YOUR SINS, LIKE YOU WASHED OUR WOUNDS.

MY SINS... I HAVE DONE SUCH EVIL, VILE THINGS. BUT I WANT TO BE CLEAN!

I WANT JESUS TO CLEAN MY SINS!

I BELIEVE! JESUS IS LORD!

LATER THAT NIGHT.

CAPTAIN SIR. THE MAGISTRATES HAVE ORDERED YOU TO LET THOSE TWO MEN GO.

TELL THE MAGISTRATES TO COME HERE THEMSELVES. WE ARE ROMAN CITIZENS! YET YOU FLOGGED US AND HELD US ILLEGALLY. THEY MUST ANSWER FOR THEIR *OWN* CRIMES!

ACTS 16:29-37

--PLEASE, GOOD SIR. SEE FIT TO FORGIVE US.

LAST NIGHT, YOU WERE NOT SO COURTEOUS!

WE DID NOT KNOW--

KNOW WHAT? OUR CITIZENSHIP? IF WE WERE NOT ROMAN, YOU WOULD SEE FIT TO BEAT US AND IMPRISON US FOR NOTHING? WE BROKE NO LAW!

YOU'RE ABSOLUTELY RIGHT. YOU WERE INNOCENT. PLEASE, WE ARE SORRY. AS MAGISTRATE I BEG YOU. JUST...GO. PLEASE.

WHY DID YOU MAKE THEM COME?

FOR THE BELIEVERS WE LEAVE BEHIND. TO PROTECT THEM. WE WERE DECLARED INNOCENT. BY PROXY, SO ARE LYDIA AND THE OTHERS.

MUST YOU GO?

OUR WOUNDS ARE HEALING. WE ARE STRONG ENOUGH TO TRAVEL.

AND THE CHURCH HERE IS STRONG ENOUGH TO THRIVE. THERE IS MUCH MORE WORK TO DO. I WILL FOREVER KEEP YOU IN MY PRAYERS.

THANK YOU FOR EVERYTHING!

MAY GOD BLESS YOU ALL!

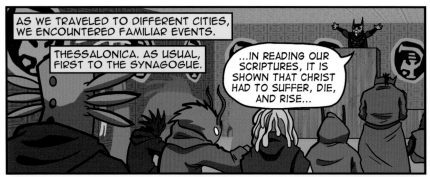

AS WE TRAVELED TO DIFFERENT CITIES, WE ENCOUNTERED FAMILIAR EVENTS.

THESSALONICA. AS USUAL, FIRST TO THE SYNAGOGUE.

...IN READING OUR SCRIPTURES, IT IS SHOWN THAT CHRIST HAD TO SUFFER, DIE, AND RISE...

SOME BELIEVED THE CHRIST'S TEACHINGS -- MAINLY DEVOUT GREEKS AND WOMEN.

SOME REJECTED THE CHRIST'S TEACHINGS...

...VIOLENTLY.

THEY DEFY CAESAR!!!

SEND OUT THE CHRISTIANS!

KILL THEM ALL!

WE WERE FORCED TO ESCAPE UNDER COVER OF DARKNESS.

BEREA. AS USUAL, FIRST TO THE SYNAGOGUE.

...CHRIST'S SUFFERING WAS WRITTEN ABOUT IN OUR SCRIPTURES HUNDREDS OF YEARS AGO...

SOME BELIEVED AND EVEN SCOURED THE SCRIPTURES TO SEE IF OUR WORDS WERE TRUE.

FANTASTIC!

"I AM POURED OUT LIKE WATER...THEY PIERCED MY HANDS AND MY FEET...THEY DIVIDE MY GARMENTS AMONG THEM, AND THROW DICE FOR MY CLOTHING....PSALM 22"[1]

SOME REJECTED THE CHRIST'S TEACHINGS...

...VIOLENTLY.

PAUL MUST BE DESTROYED!

AND, ONCE AGAIN, AN ESCAPE WAS MADE.

IT'S BETTER WE SPLIT UP, PAUL. YOU HEAD TO ATHENS AND WE'LL MEET UP WITH YOU SOON.

ACTS 17:1-15, [1]PSALM 22 (NLT)

ATHENS.

AS USUAL, FIRST TO THE SYNAGOGUE TO SPEAK TO THE JEWS ABOUT THE CHRIST.

BUT ATHENS WAS DIFFERENT. A CITY CONSUMED BY FALSE IDOLS.

COME! WORSHIP! I'VE GOT THE BEST GOLDEN GODS AND READY MADE SACRIFICES! CHEAP!

WORSHIP AND BE BLESSED!

EXCUSE ME, HAS THIS GOD EVER ANSWERED ANY OF YOUR PRAYERS?

WELL, I DON'T KNOW 'BOUT THIS ONE, BUT I MAKE SACRIFICES TO A COUPLE DOZEN EVERY WEEK.

HOW ELSE COULD I WORSHIP THE GOD IT REPRESENTS?

WHY ARE YOU BUYING THIS IDOL?

WHAT IF I TOLD YOU ABOUT A GOD THAT LISTENED WITHOUT THE NEED OF A GRAVEN IMAGE?

HEY! WE'RE DOING BUSINESS HERE!

HEY THERE, YOU'RE PAUL, HM?

UTTERLY UNBELIEVABLE.

YES. I AM. AND YOU ARE?

WE'RE EPICUREANS. WE SEEK PLEASURE BY FULFILLING OUR DESIRES.

AND *WE* ARE STOICS. WE SEEK VIRTUE BY REMOVING OUR DESIRES.

THE STOICS ARE A BUNCH OF BORING OLD-TIMERS.

AT LEAST WE ARE MINDFUL OF THE DAMAGE YOUR GLUTTONY CAUSES.

BEING MINDFUL IS FOR THE BIRDS. WHAT DO YOU THINK PAUL?

WE'VE HEARD STRANGE THINGS OF YOU, LIKE THIS "RESURRECTED GOD" NONSENSE.

WE WISH TO HEAR YOUR PHILOSOPHY.

SEE IF THERE IS ANY BIT WE CAN SYNTHESIZE INTO OUR OWN!

OH, YOU MEN OF ATHENS!

YOU ARE VERY RELIGIOUS! TOO RELIGIOUS!

LOOK AT THIS STATUE! "TO AN UNKNOWN GOD"?

YOU TALK AND TALK ABOUT IDEAS AND PHILOSOPHIES, BUT ARE STILL IGNORANT OF WHAT YOU WORSHIP!

MY GOD-- "UNKNOWN" TO YOU-- IS THE ONE TRUE GOD, WHO IN FACT CRAFTED THE WORLD AND EVERYTHING IN IT-- INCLUDING YOU!

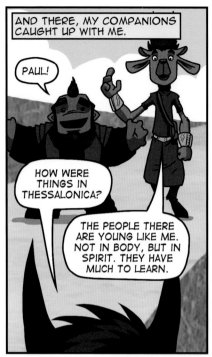

AND THERE, MY COMPANIONS CAUGHT UP WITH ME.

PAUL!

HOW WERE THINGS IN THESSALONICA?

THE PEOPLE THERE ARE YOUNG LIKE ME. NOT IN BODY, BUT IN SPIRIT. THEY HAVE MUCH TO LEARN.

I WILL WRITE THEM.

THEY WOULD APPRECIATE THAT.

THEY HAVE MANY QUESTIONS ABOUT CHRIST'S SECOND COMING.

ONCE AGAIN, WE BEGAN OUR WORK IN THE SYNAGOGUE...

--AND I STAND HERE TODAY AND TELL YOU, JESUS IS THE CHRIST OUR HOLY WRITINGS SPOKE OF!

AND ONCE AGAIN, WE WERE REJECTED.

HOW DARE YOU SPEAK YOUR FILTH IN THIS HOLY PLACE!

DON'T FOUL OUR EARS WITH YOUR VILE SPEWINGS!

AND DON'T COME BACK YOU FILTHY LIARS!

FINE! WE'LL LEAVE! BUT YOUR BLOOD IS ON YOUR OWN HEADS, NOT OURS!

THE GENTILES ARE OPEN TO THE MESSAGE OF THE MESSIAH! LET US TAKE IT TO THEM!

EXCUSE ME, PAUL? PLEASE STOP FOR A SECOND.

MY NAME IS TITIUS JUSTUS, A GOD FOLLOWER. CRISPUS, THE SYNAGOGUE RULER, HE MIGHT NOT LISTEN, BUT I WOULD HEAR MORE.

I LIVE NEARBY. WOULD YOU TEACH IN MY HOME?

AS I WAS SAYING AT THE SYNAGOGUE, JESUS OF NAZARETH IS THE CHRIST OUR HOLY WRITINGS SPEAK OF--

PROOF, SIR! I NEED PROOF!

CRISPUS!

I KNOW YOUR STORY, PAUL.

SHOW ME THE STORY OF JESUS!

AWESOME! START HERE. FROM THE PROPHET DANIEL'S WRITINGS...

THE MESSAGE PIERCED CRISPUS' HEART.

...A BLESSING, AND A COMPLICATION.

CRISPUS AND HIS FAMILY WANT TO BE BAPTIZED, NOW.

REALLY? AMAZING! THE OTHERS FROM THE SYNAGOGUE WON'T BE HAPPY ABOUT THAT!

NO. NO THEY WON'T. TIME FOR US TO LEAVE?

WE MAY BE IN DANGER, YES.

THAT NIGHT...

PAUL.

YES, LORD?

DON'T BE AFRAID! SPEAK OUT! AND DON'T BE SILENT!

FOR I AM WITH YOU.

NO ONE WILL ATTACK AND HARM YOU--

--FOR MANY PEOPLE IN THIS CITY BELONG TO ME.[1]

AND, AS USUAL, MANY DID NOT.

WE STAYED IN CORINTH FOR 18 MONTHS.

AS USUAL, MANY PEOPLE WERE TRANSFORMED BY THE HOLY SPIRIT, BELIEVING THE CHRIST'S MESSAGE.

I AM SOSTHENES, CRISPUS' REPLACEMENT AS SYNAGOGUE RULER.

COME WITH US AND WE WON'T HURT YOU.

OH, YES, I HAVE IT ON HIGH AUTHORITY THAT YOU WON'T HURT ME...

TELL ME, WHY HAVE I BEEN BROUGHT HERE?

GREAT GALLIO, WISE PROCONSUL...

THIS PAUL, HE PERSUADES PEOPLE TO WORSHIP GOD IN WAYS CONTRARY TO GOD'S LAW!

SIR, IF I MAY--

THEY DRAGGED ME TO THE GOVERNOR FOR JUDGMENT.

NO. YOU MAY *NOT!*

YOU'RE SERIOUS?

THIS PUNY RODENT'S ONLY CRIME IS RELIGIOUS DISPUTE?

GET OUT OF MY SIGHT YOU RELIGIOUS FOOLS!

YOU SHOULD BE BEATEN FOR THIS GROSS WASTE OF TIME!

WE LEFT, REVISITING EPHESUS AND SOME OTHER PLACES ON OUR WAY TO JERUSALEM FOR THE FEAST.

AND THEN...

...TO ANTIOCH.

I HAVEN'T BEEN HERE SINCE THE LAST TIME I SAW BARNABAS.

OUR STAY IN ANTIOCH WAS BOTH HOMECOMING...

...THE SPIRIT OF THE LORD HAS MOVED AMONG JEWS AND GENTILES.

...AND REUNION.

PETER! GOOD TO SEE YOU!

NOT JUST ME!

BARNABAS.

PAUL. I HAVE HEARD GOOD THINGS OF YOUR MISSION THESE PAST YEARS.

INDEED. HE HAS.

AND I YOURS. JOHN MARK HAS BEEN A GREAT HELP TO YOU, I UNDERSTAND.

EVERYONE, PLEASE!

WE HAVE A MEAL FOR YOU! YOU MUST BE HUNGRY AFTER YOUR JOURNEY!

YOU'RE GOING TO LOVE THIS!

I... I DON'T KNOW, PAUL.

I THINK WE'LL FIND SOMEWHERE ELSE TO EAT.

WHY?

THAT'S JUST NOT THE TYPE OF FOOD WE PREFER TO EAT.

YOU...

YOU HYPOCRITES!

WE'VE ALREADY *HAD* THIS CONVERSATION!

YOU'RE STILL LETTING THOSE WHO ARGUE THAT GENTILES MUST BECOME JEWISH TO DETERMINE YOUR ACTIONS?

NOW, PAUL, YOU HAD TIMOTHY BECOME JEWISH!

YES! BECAUSE HYPOCRITES LIKE YOU AND YOUR FRIENDS HERE WOULDN'T ACCEPT HIM IF HE WASN'T!

WE *ARE* JEWISH, PAUL!

WE ARE JEWISH BY BIRTH! BUT WE HAVE DIED TO THE LAW WE WERE BORN INTO!

EVEN BARNABAS HAS BEEN LED ASTRAY!

I *NEVER* THOUGHT BARNABAS COULD FALL INTO HYPOCRISY LIKE THIS!

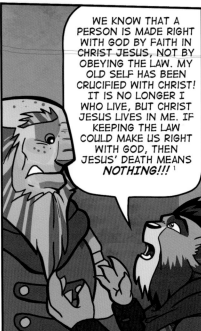

WE KNOW THAT A PERSON IS MADE RIGHT WITH GOD BY FAITH IN CHRIST JESUS, NOT BY OBEYING THE LAW. MY OLD SELF HAS BEEN CRUCIFIED WITH CHRIST! IT IS NO LONGER I WHO LIVE, BUT CHRIST JESUS LIVES IN ME. IF KEEPING THE LAW COULD MAKE US RIGHT WITH GOD, THEN JESUS' DEATH MEANS *NOTHING!!!* [1]

YOU'RE RIGHT, PAUL. YOU'RE RIGHT.

THANK YOU, PAUL.

OUR DISAGREEMENT ABOUT JOHN MARK, WE LET IT DESTROY OUR FRIENDSHIP.

BUT TODAY, YOU REBUKED ME...

...AS YOU WOULD REBUKE AN OLD FRIEND.

AS IRON SHARPENS IRON, SO WAS FELLOWSHIP WITH THE BRETHREN.

I SOON SET OFF ON MY THIRD MISSIONARY JOURNEY.

IN EPHESUS, WE FOUND TWELVE MEN WHO BELIEVED JOHN THE BAPTIST'S TEACHINGS, BUT HAD NOT YET HEARD OF JESUS.

WHEN THEY HEARD, THEY BELIEVED AND WERE BAPTIZED.

THESE MEN WERE FILLED WITH THE SPIRIT-- THEY SPOKE IN LANGUAGES THEY HAD NEVER LEARNED AND THEY PROPHESIED.

LIKE ALWAYS, SOME IN THE SYNAGOGUE NOT ONLY DID NOT BELIEVE, THEY PUBLICLY DEFAMED THE PEOPLE OF THE WAY.

IDIOTS!

BLASPHEMERS!

SO I TOOK THOSE WHO BELIEVED IN THE WAY TO A SCHOOL BELONGING TO A TEACHER CALLED TYRANNUS.

THERE, WE TAUGHT AND DEBATED AND MANY MORE PEOPLE HEARD US EXPLAIN THE WAY -- BOTH JEWS AND GREEKS.

WE BELIEVE THE GODS WILL NOT LISTEN UNLESS EVERYTHING IS WHITE AS SNOW!

THIS IS WHY WE WEAR WHITE! WE WISH OUR SOULS TO BE CLEAN AS SNOW, SO THE GODS WILL LISTEN!

BUT DON'T YOU SEE THAT IS IMPOSSIBLE! YOU'LL NEVER WASH YOURSELF PURE ON YOUR OWN...

I STAYED IN EPHESUS THREE YEARS, WORKING WHEN I WAS NOT TEACHING.

WHILE I WAS THERE...

...GOD DID MANY MIRACULOUS THINGS THROUGH MY HANDS--

--SO THAT EVEN RAGS THAT TOUCHED MY BODY--

AHA!!!

--BROUGHT HEALING?

WE TAUGHT, HEALED, AND DROVE OUT DEMONS.

SOME FRAUDS EVEN TRIED TO EMULATE US.

I COMMAND YOU, DEMON, BE GONE! IN THE NAME OF JESUS, WHOM PAUL PREACHES!

HMM-HEH. I KNOW PAUL.

I DEFINITELY KNOW JESUS.

BUT WHO ARE YOU WEASELS?

NEWS SPREAD AND GREAT RESPECT GREW FOR THE NAME OF JESUS.

AND MANY MORE CAME TO BELIEVE.

MANY SORCERERS REPENTED AND BURNED THEIR EVIL SCROLLS.

AND THE WORD OF GOD GREW.

THIS CAUSED AN UPROAR AMONG CERTAIN PEOPLE OF THE CITY.

WE'RE LOSING MONEY BY THE SECOND!!!

--THIS PAUL HAS CONVINCED PEOPLE THAT GODS CANNOT BE CRAFTED BY HANDS! THAT'S *OUR* HANDS HE'S TALKING ABOUT!

IT WAS ONLY A MATTER OF TIME BEFORE RIOTS BROKE OUT AND OUR LIVES THREATENED. LIKE ALWAYS, WE BRUSHED THE DIRT OFF OUR SHOULDERS AND MOVED ON...

...ACCOMPANIED BY A NEW GROUP OF FRIENDS.

ONCE AGAIN, I TRAVELED TO THOSE CHURCHES I HELPED START.

THESE REUNIONS WERE BLESSED TIMES.

...IN ALL THE DANGERS I HAVE FACED, IN ALL THE DANGERS *YOU* WILL FACE...

IN TROAS, WE FELLOWSHIPPED LATE INTO THE NIGHT.

...KNOW THAT NOTHING CAN SEPARATE YOU FROM THE LOVE OF GOD...

...NOTHING FROM ABOVE OR--*HE'S FALLING!!!*

NO!!!

98

PAUL... HE...HE'S DEAD!

OH, LORD JESUS, PLEASE...

PLEASE.

GIVE HIM...

...LIFE.

OH THANK JESUS!!!

WHAT... WHAT'S HAPPENING?

I HAD A DREAM... ONE OF THOSE FALLING DREAMS, YOU KNOW?

A MIRACLE!!!

PRAISE JESUS!

WHAT AN AWESOME GOD!

EVEN AFTER THAT, I PREACHED UNTIL THE SUN CAME UP.

AS I WAS SAYING, NO POWER IN THE SKY ABOVE OR IN THE EARTH BELOW - INDEED, NOTHING IN ALL CREATION WILL EVER BE ABLE TO SEPARATE US FROM THE LOVE OF GOD THAT IS REVEALED IN CHRIST JESUS OUR LORD.[1]

IN SOME WAYS, THE LATEST LEG OF MY TRAVELS FELT LIKE A FINAL FAREWELL.

I KNEW GOD WAS PREPARING ME FOR GREAT SUFFERING.

I SENT THE OTHERS AHEAD BY SHIP WHILE I WALKED.

ALONE, I STILL FOUND OPPORTUNITIES TO MINISTER AND SHARE...

...AND ALONE, I PRAYED WITHOUT CEASING.

...WHATEVER I FACE LORD, GIVE ME STRENGTH.

THROUGH YOU, I CAN DO ALL THINGS...

I MET THE OTHERS IN ASSOS.

WHERE TO NOW, PAUL?

TO EPHESUS AND THEN...

...TO JERUSALEM.

IN EPHESUS...

PAUL!

I NEED TO SPEAK WITH YOU MY BROTHERS.

SINCE STEPPING FOOT IN YOUR LAND, YOU KNOW HOW I'VE LIVED...

...SERVING THE LORD HUMBLY AND WITHOUT FEAR.

NOW, I'M CALLED TO JERUSALEM, WHERE IT ALL BEGAN.

I DON'T KNOW WHAT WAITS FOR ME THERE, EXCEPT THAT GOD'S HOLY SPIRIT HAS TOLD ME I FACE PRISON AND AFFLICTION.

ACTS 20:13-23

BUT PRISON AND TORTURE DO NOT FRIGHTEN ME.

I MUST COMPLETE THE RACE THE LORD HAS SET BEFORE ME.

MANY YEARS AGO, THE LORD GAVE ME A TASK MORE IMPORTANT THAN MY OWN LIFE.

SPREADING THE GOOD NEWS OF CHRIST JESUS, OUR LORD AND SAVIOR!

MOST OF YOU WILL NOT SEE ME AGAIN. SO I SAY TO YOU, TAKE CARE OF THE CHURCH OF GOD. AFTER I LEAVE, FALSE TEACHERS WILL JOIN THE CHURCH AND SPREAD LIES ABOUT JESUS.

BE ON YOUR GUARD.

THIS CANNOT BE TRUE!

NEVER SEE YOU AGAIN?!

I KNEW THEY WOULD NOT WANT ME TO LEAVE THEM...

HAVE YOU EVER THOUGHT, MAYBE GOD TOLD YOU OF THE TROUBLE YOU'D FACE IN JERUSALEM AS A WARNING?!

...BUT IT WAS NOT THEIR WILL I FOLLOWED.

A WARNING?

YES. IT IS A WARNING.

AND AS I TRAVELED TOWARD JERUSALEM, I FOUND THAT GOD DID NOT JUST GIVE THE WARNING TO ME!

ACTS 20:24-38

AND THUS SAYS THE HOLY SPIRIT!

THIS IS WHAT THE LEADERS IN JERUSALEM WILL DO!

STOP!

THEY WILL TIE YOU UP AND TURN YOU OVER TO THE GENTILES.

GET OFF HIM, YOU LUNATIC!!!

TIMOTHY, I'VE HEARD OF THIS MAN. HE'S A PROPHET. HIS WORDS, THEY ARE NOT HIS OWN!

YOU UNDERSTAND WHAT AWAITS YOU?

I DO.

AND YOU INSIST ON RETURNING TO JERUSALEM?

I DO.

THERE'S NO STOPPING YOU, IS THERE?

I MUST GO. IN THE NAME OF THE LORD JESUS, I AM WILLING TO GO IF IT MEANS PRISON.

OR DEATH.

THESE WARNINGS, THEY ARE NOT TO *STOP* ME FROM GOING. THEY ARE TO *PREPARE* ME FOR WHAT I FACE IN GOING. BUT I AM STILL GOING.

THE LORD'S WILL BE DONE!

AND I RETURNED TO JERUSALEM...

JERUSALEM.

IF I HADN'T GONE THERE, I WOULDN'T HAVE ENDED UP HERE.

HERE, INSIDE THIS CELL.

WHERE I AWAIT THE WILL OF GOD TO UNFOLD...

...WHILE PERSECUTION FOR CHRISTIANS GROWS OUTSIDE...

DID YOU HEED THE CRIES OF THE WOMEN AND CHILDREN DEVOURED IN THE FIRE YOU COWARDLY WORMS SET!?!

...AS NERO ACCUSES US OF A HORRENDOUS CRIME...

PLEASE! PLEASE DON'T DO THIS!

...AND PUNISHES MY BROTHERS AND SISTERS, EN MASSE.

WE GIVE PRAISE TO THE LORD, EVEN NOW!

ONLY RIGHT THEY BURN, AFTER WHAT THEY DID TO ROME!

WELL, DID NOT THEIR "LORD" SAY HE WAS "THE WAY, THE TRUTH, AND THE LIGHT"?

THE LIGHT! IF NOT FOR THE WORLD, AT LEAST FOR THIS MEAL! PASS THE MUTTON...

LUKE HAS JUST GIVEN ME THIS LETTER FROM PAUL.

I WANTED TO SHARE THIS ENCOURAGEMENT: "NEVER BE ASHAMED TO TELL OTHERS ABOUT OUR LORD. AND DON'T BE ASHAMED OF ME...WITH THE STRENGTH GOD GIVES YOU, BE READY TO SUFFER WITH ME FOR THE SAKE OF THE GOOD NEWS."[1]

BUT IN SPITE OF FACING PERSECUTION...

...THE CHURCH SURVIVES AND GROWS STRONGER.

I PRAY FOR THE CHURCH WITHOUT CEASING. I LONG FOR THE DAY I SEE THEM AGAIN. I LONG FOR THE DAY I SEE CHRIST JESUS AGAIN! LORD, FILL ME WITH JOY AS I FACE HARDSHIP, PERSECUTION--

--AND EVEN, DEATH.

[1] 2 TIMOTHY 1:8 (NLT)

CHAPTER THREE: THE GOOD FIGHT

HE WILL SWALLOW UP DEATH FOREVER!

THE SOVEREIGN LORD WILL WIPE AWAY ALL TEARS.

HE WILL REMOVE FOREVER ALL INSULTS AND MOCKERY

AGAINST HIS LAND AND PEOPLE.

THE LORD HAS SPOKEN!

–ISAIAH 25:8 (NLT)

I KNEW, OF COURSE, AS SOON AS I FOLLOWED THE CHRIST JESUS, WHAT OTHER END COULD THERE BE?

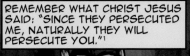

REMEMBER WHAT CHRIST JESUS SAID: "SINCE THEY PERSECUTED ME, NATURALLY THEY WILL PERSECUTE YOU."[1]

I'VE GOT SOMETHING FOR YOU.

YOU'RE LUCKY WE LIKE YOU, OR YOU'D NEVER GET THIS.

THANK YOU.

BAH! DON'T MENTION IT!

I MEAN IT, DON'T MENTION IT! DON'T WANT ANYONE THINKING WE'RE GOING SOFT HERE, YEAH?

OF COURSE NOT.

Y'KNOW, IT'S TRUTH THAT SOME OF YOU CHRISTIANS ADMITTED TO THE FIRE--

UNDER TORTURE!

OF COURSE UNDER TORTURE! HOW ELSE? ANYWAY, AFTER MEETIN' YOU GUYS, YOU'RE NOT SO BAD!

I MEAN, YOU'VE BEEN NUTHIN' BUT KIND TO ME. ME, THE ONE WHO ESCORTS YOU TO YOUR BEATIN'S!

I HAVE TOLD YOU, MY LORD WANTS ME TO--

--"LOVE YOUR NEIGHBOR AS YOURSELF," I KNOW.[2]

IT'S A STUPID WAY TO LIVE!

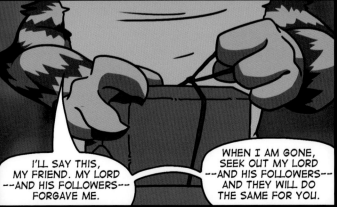

I'LL SAY THIS, MY FRIEND. MY LORD --AND HIS FOLLOWERS-- FORGAVE ME.

WHEN I AM GONE, SEEK OUT MY LORD --AND HIS FOLLOWERS-- AND THEY WILL DO THE SAME FOR YOU.

THANK GOD...

[1] JOHN 15:20 (NLT), [2] MARK 12:31 (NLT)

MY CLOAK! BUT, THAT CAN ONLY MEAN--

PAUL!

PAUL, WE DON'T HAVE MUCH TIME!

TIMOTHY! I BEGAN TO LOSE HOPE I'D SEE YOU!

OI!

NO PASSING NOTHING! WE GIVED 'IM HIS CAPE OR WHATEVER! THAT'S ALL!

SORRY. WE DIDN'T HAVE ENOUGH BRIBE MONEY FOR ONE OF US TO GET IN, LET ALONE ALL THREE.

BUT WE HAD ENOUGH TO SPEAK TO YOU LIKE THIS. WE ONLY HAVE A FEW MINUTES, THOUGH.

IT IS GREAT TO SEE YOU, OLD FRIEND!

AND YOU!

YOU ARE A TREASURE, PAUL. YOUR CHAINS INSPIRE US. KNOW WE WILL CONTINUE TO PREACH WITHOUT FEAR.

ALRIGHT, ALRIGHT! TIME'S UP YOU STINKIN' CHRISTIANS.

PAUL! WE WILL COME AGAIN SOON. WE LOVE YOU PAUL!

I...I'M SORRY.

NO, DO NOT BE.

THIS WAS MORE THAN I HOPED FOR. I THANK YOU.

TIME PASSES SLOWLY IN PRISON.

THE WAITING. THE ANTICIPATION.

I TELL YOU THE TRUTH, I AM JOYFUL DESPITE MY CHAINS.

I REJOICE NOT ONLY IN MY FUTURE IN HEAVEN, BUT ALSO IN THE JOURNEY THAT LED ME HERE...

...THE JOURNEY BACK TO WHERE IT ALL BEGAN: JERUSALEM.

PAUL, PAUL, PAUL! I AM SO GLAD YOU CAME! MANY PEOPLE WISH TO TALK WITH YOU!

OF COURSE! TOMORROW.

TONIGHT, LET US CATCH UP, EH?

INCLUDING JAMES AND THE OTHER ELDERS. THERE ARE A FEW PROBLEMS THAT NEED TO BE SORTED.

IT'S NOT JAMES AND THE ELDERS I'M WORRIED ABOUT. I SERIOUSLY DOUBT *THEY'RE* GOING TO PUT PAUL IN SHACKLES. STILL, WE SHOULD BE ON OUR GUARD.

THAT DOESN'T SOUND GOOD.

SO, DOCTOR LUKE, THIS IS JERUSALEM! TO THINK, THE CHRIST WALKED THESE VERY STREETS.

I NEVER THOUGHT OF IT THAT WAY, TROPHIMUS.

AS AN EPHESIAN AND A --HOW YOU CALL IT-- GENTILE, I FIND IT QUITE INSPIRING TO BE HERE!

THAT NIGHT.

...AND RIGHT IN THE MIDDLE OF MY SERMON, HE FELL ASLEEP AND FELL RIGHT OUT THE WINDOW!

WAS HE OKAY?

NO! THE BOY *DIED!!!*

BUT PAUL PRAYED AND GOD BREATHED LIFE BACK INTO HIM!

AFTER THAT, WE'VE BEEN CAREFUL TO STAY AWAKE NO MATTER HOW LONG-WINDED PAUL GETS!

THE NEXT DAY WAS QUITE DIFFERENT.

THAT'S A LIE! I SHOULD KNOW!

PAUL, GOD HAS CERTAINLY BLESSED YOUR WORK WITH THE GENTILES.

AYE, BUT A DIVISION GROWS BETWEEN THE JEWISH AND THE GENTILE BELIEVERS! WORD HAS SPREAD THAT YOU TELL JEWS IN GENTILE CITIES TO TURN AWAY FROM MOSES' LAW!

HOW CAN I HELP BRIDGE THIS DIVIDE?

WE'VE WRITTEN TO THE GENTILES, EXPLAINING THAT THEY DO NOT NEED TO FOLLOW THE LAW OF MOSES.

AND YOU'VE SAID --AND WE AGREE-- THAT FOLLOWING THE LAW OF MOSES DOES NOT GIVE US SALVATION, BUT THAT THE LAW OF MOSES CAN STILL BE FOLLOWED.

NO ONE WANTS DIVISION.

THE CHRIST HAS UNITED JEWS AND GENTILES UNDER HIS NEW COVENANT. SINCE YOU ARE A JEW, BUT YOU ALSO REPRESENT IN MANY WAYS THE GENTILES, IT WOULD MEAN A LOT IF THE BELIEVERS HERE COULD SEE THAT YOU STILL KEEP THE LAW.

TIMOTHY IS RIGHT.

I HAVE NEVER SAID SUCH THINGS.

THERE ARE FOUR MEN AMONG US WHO WISH TO TAKE THE NAZIRITE VOW... I UNDERSTAND YOU ONCE PLANNED TO TAKE THAT VOW BUT DID NOT MAKE IT BACK TO JERUSALEM.

YES.

TAKE THE NAZIRITE VOW NOW, WITH THEM. THEY CANNOT AFFORD SOME OF THE COSTS, BUT--

I'LL COVER IT, NO PROBLEM.

THE NEXT DAY.

I DO NOT UNDERSTAND THIS "VOW."

IT IS A VOW OF PURIFICATION FROM SIN. OF SEPARATION FROM THE WORLD. OF CONSECRATION TO GOD.

YEAH. DON'T UNDERSTAND.

YOU SAID THAT THE BLOOD OF CHRIST IS ALL THE SACRIFICE NEEDED.

TRUE. MY HOPE IS THAT BOTH JEWS AND GENTILES WILL NOT SEE THIS VOW AS SOMETHING ALL MUST DO...

...BUT THAT, WE WOULD *ALL* GIVE OUR BODIES TO GOD AS A LIVING AND HOLY SACRIFICE.

A SPIRITUAL ACT OF WORSHIP.

THIS VOW IS A PHYSICAL ACT THAT SYMBOLIZES A SPIRITUAL TRUTH.

SO, FOR THE NEXT SEVEN DAYS, I WILL BE SYMBOLICALLY PURIFIED.

UNFORTUNATELY, GENTILES ARE NOT ALLOWED TO ENTER THE TEMPLE.

AH, BUT SEE, I DO NOT WORRY MYSELF ABOUT THAT!

I MAY NOT BE WELCOME IN YOUR TEMPLE...BUT I AM WELCOME INTO CHRIST'S BODY!

ACTS 21:23-26

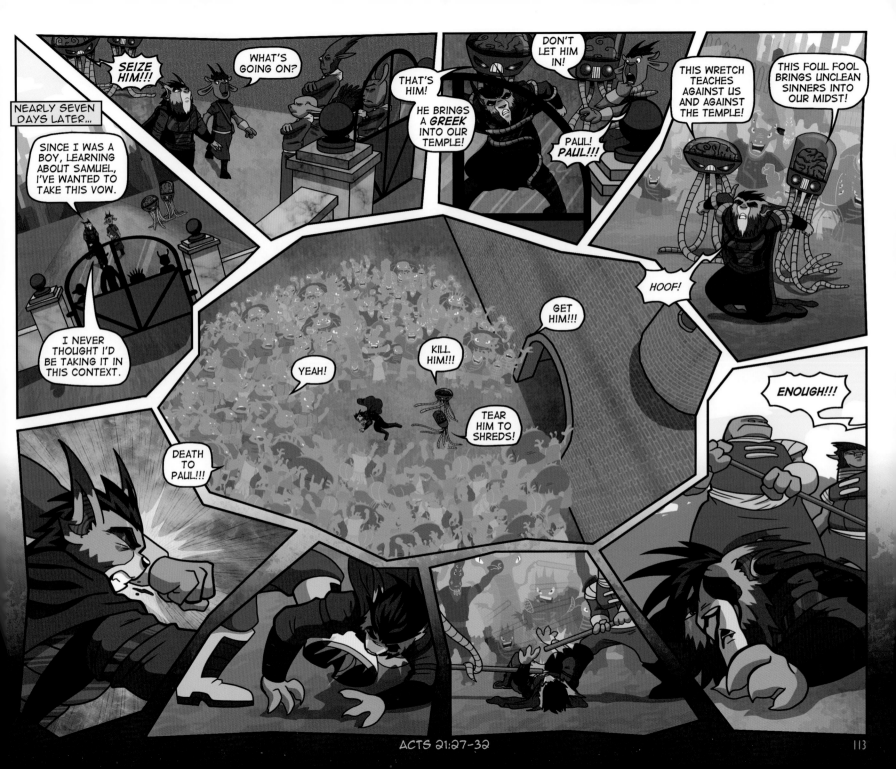

YOU WILL ALL LEAVE. *NOW!!!*

I WANT HIM CHAINED.

WHO ARE YOU? WHAT HAVE YOU DONE?

HE'S A ZEALOT!

HE WOULD TEAR DOWN THE TEMPLE!

SHUT UP!!! I DID NOT ADDRESS ANYONE BUT HIM!!!

BRING HIM INSIDE.

YES! TAKE HIM!

KILL HIM!

DESIST AND DISPERSE!

BE THANKFUL I DON'T TAKE YOU ALL IN FOR THIS MOB ACTION!

HAVE HIM SCOURGED, THEN--

EXCUSE ME...

MAY I SAY SOMETHING?

YOU... YOU SPEAK GREEK FLAWLESSLY!

I THOUGHT YOU WERE THAT EGYPTIAN TERRORIST...

THE ONE WHO GATHERED A FEW THOUSAND PEOPLE IN THE WILDERNESS, YOU SEE, AND I...

WHO ARE YOU?

I AM PAUL, A JEW BUT ALSO A CITIZEN OF TARSUS IN CILICIA.

JEWISH, EH? YOUR PEOPLE DON'T SEEM TO LIKE YOU MUCH.

MAY I SPEAK TO THEM?

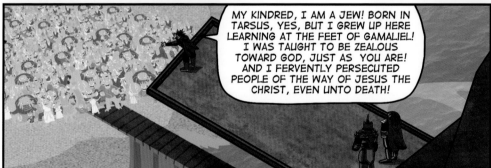

MY KINDRED, I AM A JEW! BORN IN TARSUS, YES, BUT I GREW UP HERE LEARNING AT THE FEET OF GAMALIEL! I WAS TAUGHT TO BE ZEALOUS TOWARD GOD, JUST AS YOU ARE! AND I FERVENTLY PERSECUTED PEOPLE OF THE WAY OF JESUS THE CHRIST, EVEN UNTO DEATH!

AND WHILE I DID SO -- AS YOU DID TO ME TODAY -- I CRASHED HEADFIRST INTO THE CHRIST JESUS ON THE ROAD TO DAMASCUS! I WAS CONSUMED BY A HEAVENLY BALL OF LIGHT AND HE SPOKE TO ME! HE CONFIRMED HE WAS THE CHRIST! AND SO I WAS BAPTIZED! I BECAME A FOLLOWER OF HIS WAY AND I'VE SHARED IT WITH THE WORLD-- TO BOTH JEW AND GENTILE!

FOOL!

KILL THE HERETIC! KILL THE HERETIC!

TAKE HIM AWAY!

WHAT'D HE SAY? WHY DO THESE PEOPLE HATE HIM? HAVE HIM SCOURGED AND QUESTIONED.

LISTEN, IS IT LEGAL TO SCOURGE A ROMAN CITIZEN?

ESPECIALLY A ROMAN CITIZEN WHO HAS BEEN CONDEMNED OF NO CRIME?

UH, CAPTAIN?

IS THIS TRUE? I PAID A *LOT* OF CASH FOR MY ROMAN CITIZENSHIP.

I WAS BORN FREE.

TAKE HIM DOWN.

HE WILL FACE HIS ACCUSERS TOMORROW!

AND SO, AFTER ALL THESE YEARS, I FINALLY FOUND MYSELF AS PART OF THE SANHEDRIN'S OFFICIAL PROCEEDINGS.

KINDRED, I HAVE LIVED IN GOOD CONSCIENCE--

SILENCE HIM! STRIKE HIS MOUTH!

GOD WILL STRIKE *YOU*! FOR YOU JUDGE ME BY THE LAW, BUT BREAK IT YOURSELF!

YOU DARE INSULT GOD'S HIGH PRIEST?

I APOLOGIZE. I DIDN'T REALIZE. I SHOULD NOT HAVE SAID THAT.

FOR IT IS WRITTEN, "YOU MUST NOT SPEAK EVIL OF ANY OF YOUR RULERS."[1]

I KNEW I WOULD NOT GET A FAIR TRIAL HERE, BEFORE THE PHARISEES AND SADDUCEES WHO MADE UP THE SANHEDRIN.

BUT IT WAS THEN WHEN I REALIZED WHAT THAT MEANT. THE TWO FACTIONS OF THE SANHEDRIN.

PHARISEES, WHO BELIEVE IN RESURRECTION.

SADDUCEES, WHO DO NOT.

ACTS 22:24-30, ACTS 23:1-5, ACTS 23:5 (NLT)

LISTEN TO ME! I AM A PHARISEE! THE SON OF A PHARISEE! I STAND BEFORE YOU ALL, WHEN IT COMES DOWN TO IT, BECAUSE OF MY BELIEF IN *RESURRECTION!*

WHY SHOULD *THAT* BE CALLED INTO QUESTION?

HOW COULD *ANYONE* BELIEVE THAT?

AS A PHARISEE MYSELF, I FIND NO EVIL IN THIS MAN! AN ANGEL OR SPIRIT MIGHT HAVE SPOKEN TO HIM.

HE CLAIMS A DEAD MAN SPOKE TO HIM! EVERY SADDUCEE KNOWS THAT'S IMPOSSIBLE BECAUSE DEATH IS FINAL!

STOP THIS MADNESS! I BRING HIM TO ANSWER TO YOU AND THIS IS WHAT HAPPENS? TAKE THE ROMAN JEW BACK TO THE FORTRESS! IT'S A MADHOUSE! A MADHOUSE!!!

THAT NIGHT...

PAUL.

HEAR ME...

BE ENCOURAGED, PAUL. JUST AS YOU HAVE BEEN A WITNESS TO ME HERE IN JERUSALEM...

...YOU MUST PREACH THE GOOD NEWS IN ROME AS WELL.[1]

ROME. YES.

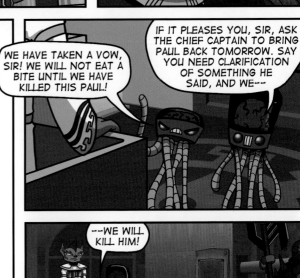

WE HAVE TAKEN A VOW, SIR! WE WILL NOT EAT A BITE UNTIL WE HAVE KILLED THIS PAUL!

IF IT PLEASES YOU, SIR, ASK THE CHIEF CAPTAIN TO BRING PAUL BACK TOMORROW. SAY YOU NEED CLARIFICATION OF SOMETHING HE SAID, AND WE--

--WE WILL KILL HIM!

ACTS 23:6-15, [1]ACTS 23:11 (NLT)

ACTS 23:16-33

NICE. JUST WHAT I WANTED.

I CAN EXPLAIN...

WHAT PROVINCE ARE YOU FROM?

CILICIA.

FINE. FINE. I WILL LISTEN TO YOU WHEN YOUR ACCUSERS COME BEFORE ME.

FIVE DAYS LATER, MY ACCUSERS ARRIVED --THE HIGH PRIEST, ANANIAS, AND A LAWYER, TERTULLUS.

GREAT AND HONORED FELIX, WORDS CANNOT EXPRESS OUR APPRECIATION FOR THE PEACE YOU BRING TO THIS NATION! WE APPRECIATE ALL THAT YOU AND YOUR FELLOW ROMANS, BUT ESPECIALLY YOU, DO FOR US!

WE DON'T WANT TO TAKE UP TOO MUCH OF YOUR VALUABLE TIME.

AND YET, HERE WE ARE.

THE PEACE YOU BRING US IS DISTURBED, HOWEVER, BY THIS MAN! HE STIRS UP RIOTS AND MOBS AND SEDITION! HE PROFANES OUR HOLY TEMPLE! WE TOOK HIM, ACCORDING TO OUR LAW, BUT THE CHIEF CAPTAIN VIOLENTLY STOPPED US!

WE COULD HAVE HANDLED THINGS, BUT THE CHIEF CAPTAIN WOULD HAVE US TAKE UP YOUR PRECIOUS TIME.

AND SO, WE HAVE COME --AT HIS REQUEST-- TO YOUR COURT.

AND YOU, DO YOU WISH TO SPEAK FOR YOURSELF?

YES, GLADLY, FOR I KNOW YOU ARE A FAIR JUDGE. MY DEFENSE IS SIMPLE: THEY CAN'T PROVE ANYTHING THEY'RE SAYING!

IN MY TIME IN JERUSALEM, I ARGUED WITH NO ONE. I STIRRED UP NO CROWDS, LET ALONE RIOTS.

I DO ADMIT TO BEING A FOLLOWER OF THE WAY, WHICH MEANS I WORSHIP THE GOD OF OUR ANCESTORS AND BELIEVE IN THE LAW AND THE PROPHETS.

HMMM. I KNOW OF THE WAY.

WHEN COMMANDER LYSIAS COMES, I WILL DECIDE THE CASE! UNTIL THEN...

"...LET PAUL HAVE FREEDOM OF THIS MANSION..."

"...AND LET HIS FRIENDS, IF HE HAS ANY, TEND TO HIM IF HE NEEDS ANYTHING ELSE!"

ALSO, A CLOAK FOR YOU, IN CASE IT GETS COLD. SO THIS IS PRISON LIFE? I BET PETER WOULDN'T *LET* THE ANGEL RESCUE HIM FROM THIS!

I'VE GOT SOME WRITING MATERIALS FOR YOU, AND A COPY OF MY LIFE OF CHRIST. I ALSO WANT TO INTERVIEW YOU FOR A SECOND VOLUME I WANT TO DO, ABOUT THE CHURCH AFTER CHRIST.

LET'S TALK, LUKE, WHILE WE STILL CAN.

AFTER A WHILE, I WAS SUMMONED TO APPEAR BEFORE FELIX AND HIS JEWISH WIFE, DRUSILLA.

HELLO! PAUL, COME! SIT! EAT!

TELL ME ABOUT THIS WAY AND WHY IT HAS GOTTEN YOU INTO TROUBLE.

I SHOULD BE RELEASED BY NOW.

BUT PERHAPS I HAVE BEEN HELD HERE FOR SUCH A TIME AS THIS.

I SPOKE TO THEM OF RIGHTEOUSNESS, SELF-CONTROL, AND JUDGMENT. TIMELY TOPICS, CONSIDERING THE RUMORS OF CORRUPTION THAT SURROUNDED THEM.

FELIX AND DRUSILLA UNDERSTOOD THE TRUTH. AND IT CHILLED THEM.

HM. YES. WELL. THANK YOU, PAUL. THIS WAS VERY ENLIGHTENING.

WHEN THE TIME IS CONVENIENT, I'LL CALL FOR YOU AGAIN.

FOR TWO YEARS, I WAS A PRISONER THERE AND A FREQUENT GUEST OF FELIX. HE WAS ALWAYS HOPING FOR A BRIBE FROM MY FELLOW FOLLOWERS OF THE WAY? WHEN FELIX WAS RELIEVED OF HIS POSITION FOR CORRUPTION AND PORCIUS FESTUS TOOK OVER...

...FELIX, EVER THE CANNY POLITICIAN, KEPT ME IMPRISONED "AS A FAVOR TO THE JEWS."

AND SO, *URMMM*, THE QUESTION BEFORE US TODAY IS WHAT TO DO WITH HIM?

SO YOU GUYS WANT TO TAKE PAUL BACK TO JERUSALEM AND TRY HIM FOR SOME STUPID RELIGIOUS DISPUTE?

FELIX DIDN'T LET YOU BECAUSE OF SOME SORT OF ASSASSINATION PLOT.

ASSASSINATION. *URMMM.* THAT'S NOT VERY NICE. AND FELIX DID NOTHING, SO NOW IT'S MY RESPONSIBILITY. ALSO NOT VERY NICE.

THIS MAN INCITES REBELLION! REBELLION AGAINST THE KING ROME HAS GIVEN US! AND THEREFORE, REBELLION AGAINST ROME!

I BROKE NO LAW. NOT CAESAR'S LAW. AND NOT MOSES' LAW.

GREAT! GRAND! GLORIOUS! THEN JUST GO TO JERUSALEM WITH THEM, STAND TRIAL, AND *URMMM,* BE FOUND INNOCENT! I'D BE HAPPY, THEY'D BE HAPPY, AND AFTERWARDS, YOU'D BE HAPPY...IF THEY FIND YOU INNOCENT, THAT IS.

NO.

NO?

NO. IF I AM TO BE TRIED, I SHOULD BE TRIED BEFORE CAESAR'S COURT!

THE CHARGES THEY LEVEL AGAINST ME ARE NOT TRUE.

I APPEAL TO CAESAR!

URRRM. OF COURSE YOU WOULD. THIS ISN'T GOING TO BE EASY, IS IT?

A FEW DAYS LATER, I FOUND MYSELF APPEARING BEFORE FESTUS AND KING HEROD AGRIPPA.

OKAY. SO. THE PLAN IS TO SEND PAUL TO ROME.

BUT FIRST, HEROD AGRIPPA, KING OF THE REGION, WANTS TO HEAR MORE.

YES. SPEAK FOR YOURSELF, PAUL. I WOULD HEAR YOU.

YES, MY BROTHER AND I ARE CURIOUS.

I'M PLEASED TO EXPLAIN MYSELF TO YOU, KING AGRIPPA. YOU ARE AN EXPERT OF JEWISH CUSTOMS AND IDEAS, SO YOU WILL UNDERSTAND WHAT I AM ACCUSED OF.

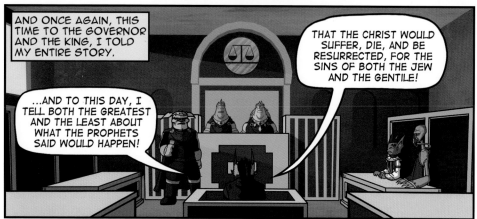

AND ONCE AGAIN, THIS TIME TO THE GOVERNOR AND THE KING, I TOLD MY ENTIRE STORY.

...AND TO THIS DAY, I TELL BOTH THE GREATEST AND THE LEAST ABOUT WHAT THE PROPHETS SAID WOULD HAPPEN!

THAT THE CHRIST WOULD SUFFER, DIE, AND BE RESURRECTED, FOR THE SINS OF BOTH THE JEW AND THE GENTILE!

RESURRECTED? FROM THE DEAD? URM, YOU'RE A SMART GUY, BUT I THINK YOUR SMARTS MAY HAVE TURNED YOU INSANE IN THE BRAIN!

NO, SIR. I SPEAK THE TRUTH. KING AGRIPPA KNOWS THESE THINGS. HE BELIEVES THE PROPHETS. I KNOW HE DOES...DON'T YOU?

INDEED. AND I ALMOST BELIEVE YOU. YOU'VE ALMOST PERSUADED ME TO BE A CHRISTIAN, AS THEY CALL YOU.

THIS MAN HAS DONE NOTHING WORTHY OF DEATH OR IMPRISONMENT. TOO BAD HE APPEALED TO CAESAR. WE COULD SET HIM FREE INSTEAD OF SENDING HIM--

ACTS 25:13-27, ACTS 26

"--TO ROME."

IT WAS A LONG JOURNEY AND THE WIND WAS AGAINST US.

WE MADE MANY STOPS ALONG THE WAY. IT MIGHT HAVE FELT EVEN LONGER IF THEY HADN'T ALLOWED LUKE TO TRAVEL WITH ME.

WHEN WE REACHED LYCIA, WE WERE FORCED TO FIND A NEW SHIP.

WORD IS YOU'RE SAILING FOR ITALY? WE MUST COME WITH YOU. I'M TRANSPORTING THIS PRISONER TO ROME.

AYE, WE'VE GOT PRISONERS ALREADY! WHAT'S ONE MORE?

THE NEW SHIP HAD A STURDY HULL AND A STURDY CAPTAIN. BUT THE NORTH WINDS GREW STRONGER STILL...

HOW MANY DAYS MORE CAN THE WINDS BE AGAINST US?

I HATE TO SAY THIS, BUT WE'RE HEADING INTO TROUBLE. THE SHIP IS IN DANGER... PERHAPS OUR VERY LIVES.

NONSENSE. THE CAPTAIN SAYS THIS HAPPENS SOMETIMES. IT'LL PASS.

PLEASE! TELL THE CAPTAIN TO LAND ON THE ISLAND OF CRETE! WE CAN WINTER THERE AND THEN GO TO ROME WHEN IT'S SAFE!

HA! YOU'RE JUST AFRAID OF FACING CAESAR! WE FOLLOW THE CAPTAIN'S ORDERS. HE HAS LOOKED TO THE SKIES AND--

AND I HAVE LOOKED TO GOD!

THE CLOUDS HID THE STARS AND THE SUN FOR MANY DAYS.

OH, LORD, YOU CALMED THE STORMS FOR PETER. HOW ABOUT NOW?

FEAR NOT, PAUL.

THE WHOLE CREW WILL SURVIVE THIS, PAUL, BECAUSE YOU *WILL* APPEAR BEFORE THE CAESAR.

IT HAS BEEN ORDAINED.

BUT THE SHIP WILL BE LOST.

AN... ANGEL?

I'D TRUST HIM, CAPTAIN.

HRMM. AYE. I DO.

THAT'S WHY I'M NOT WORRIED. AND NEITHER SHOULD YOU BE. ALL WE HAVE TO DO IS RUN AGROUND.

TWO WEEKS PASSED.

STILL NO ISLAND! WHERE'S YOUR ISLAND, PAUL? WE'RE HUNGRY! WE'RE TIRED!

CAPTAIN! WE HAVE SOME READINGS OF THE SEA BOTTOM! THE SEA FLOOR IS SLOWLY AND STEADILY RISING!

AYE?

WE COULD ALMOST WEIGH ANCHOR, SIR!

AYE!

DROP ANCHORS! SLOW THIS SHIP DOWN, BOYS!

ACTS 27:30-40

"...THE ISLAND!"

THIS ISLAND IS INHABITED. RULED BY PUBLIUS, I BELIEVE.

WHO GOES THERE?

MY NAME IS PAUL. OUR SHIP, IT CRASHED.

I KNOW THESE THINGS. BUT I DON'T KNOW YOU.

YOU ARE COLD AND RAIN IS APPROACHING.

COME WITH ME. COME *NOW!*

LUKE, TELL THE OTHERS TO FOLLOW! I THINK...

"...WE HAVE FOUND SOME FRIENDS!"

HOW DO YOU PLAN TO DO IT?

DO WHAT?

EXPLAIN TO THESE ISLANDERS THE MESSAGE OF THE CHRIST.

I KNOW IT'S WHAT YOU'RE THINKING.

I'M SURE THE OPPORTUNITY WILL COME.

FOR NOW, I'M JUST HAPPY THAT THE DANGER IS FINALLY OVER...

PUBLIUS WELCOMED US INTO HIS HOME FOR THREE DAYS.

THE LOCALS SAY YOU'RE A GOD--

--WHAT DO YOU SAY?

I'M NOT. OBVIOUSLY. I JUST FOLLOW THE ONE TRUE GOD.

INDEED. I NEED YOU. YOUR GOD, I MEAN. OR RATHER...

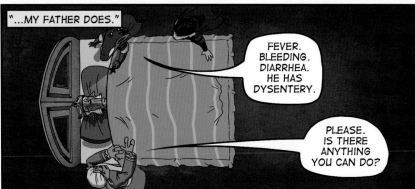

"...MY FATHER DOES."

FEVER. BLEEDING. DIARRHEA. HE HAS DYSENTERY.

PLEASE. IS THERE ANYTHING YOU CAN DO?

WHAT IS HE DOING?

PRAYING.

ABOUT WHAT?

YOUR FATHER, I WOULD ASSUME.

YES. I CAN HEAL HIM.

IN THE NAME OF JESUS CHRIST, HEAL THIS MAN!

PUBLIUS?

FATHER?

OTHERS WERE HEALED ON THAT ISLAND.

AFTER THREE MONTHS, I ONCE MORE HEADED TO ROME.

130

ACTS 28:7-10

IN ROME, I WAS AGAIN PUT INTO THE CUSTODY OF A CENTURION. I DID NOT EXPECT TO BE GIVEN SUCH FREEDOM. BUT I USED IT!

--I'D LIKE TO MEET WITH THE JEWISH LEADERS.

THERE AREN'T MANY SINCE BEING RUN OUT OF THE CITY. THERE'S AN UNDERSTANDABLE RELUCTANCE TO RETURN. BESIDES...

...AREN'T THOSE GUYS THE TYPE WHO GOT YOU INTO THIS IN THE FIRST PLACE?

I WISH TO SPEAK TO THEM.

STILL FOLLOWING THE SAME METHODS, EVEN IN PRISON...

...ADDRESSING FIRST THE JEWS, THEN THE GENTILES?

ALWAYS.

THREE DAYS LATER.

...WHICH IS WHY I CALLED YOU HERE! I AM IN CHAINS FOR SHARING ISRAEL'S HOPE WITH THE PEOPLE OF ISRAEL!

WE'VE HEARD OF THIS "WAY" OF CHRISTIANS, THOUGH.

WE'VE HEARD NOTHING OF THIS FROM JERUSALEM!

I THINK SOME OF US WOULD LIKE TO HEAR MORE...

AND I EXPLAINED THE WAY OF THE CHRIST TO THE JEWS OF ROME, FROM MORNING...

...IN THE FIRST WORDS OF THE TORAH, WE FIND PROPHECIES OF A MESSIAH...

...TO EVENING. AND SOME BELIEVED, WHILE OTHERS DID NOT.

...AND JESUS FULFILLED THE MANY PROPHECIES FOUND IN DANIEL'S WRITINGS AS WELL, WHERE IT SAYS...

FOR TWO YEARS, I LIVED IN THAT HOUSE. I WROTE LETTERS, RECEIVED GUESTS, AND PREACHED THE GOSPEL OPENLY.

WE MUST BE IMITATORS OF GOD AND LIVE A LIFE OF LOVE.

AND I KEPT APPRISED OF THE NEWS OF THE CHURCH.

WE WANTED TO BRING YOU THE NEWS OURSELVES.

BARNABAS... OH, BARNABAS...

DETAILS ARE SKETCHY, BUT IT IS OBVIOUS HE WAS KILLED FOR PREACHING THE GOSPEL.

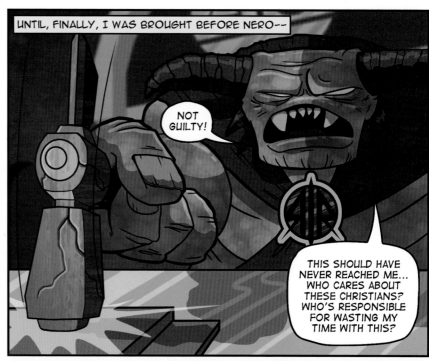

UNTIL, FINALLY, I WAS BROUGHT BEFORE NERO--

NOT GUILTY!

THIS SHOULD HAVE NEVER REACHED ME... WHO CARES ABOUT THESE CHRISTIANS? WHO'S RESPONSIBLE FOR WASTING MY TIME WITH THIS?

IT SEEMED TOO GOOD TO BE TRUE. I KNEW GOD HAD OTHER PLANS.

THANK YOU, PAUL. YOU SHOULDN'T HAVE BEEN HERE IN THE FIRST PLACE. BUT I'M GLAD YOU WERE. TWO YEARS, ASSIGNED TO YOU? WHATEVER'S NEXT CAN'T COMPARE.

I JUST HOPE YOU REMEMBER THE THINGS YOU OVERHEARD!

REUNITED WITH OLD FRIENDS, WE SET ABOUT PREACHING THE GOSPEL EVERYWHERE.

BUT NOT LONG AFTER MY RELEASE...

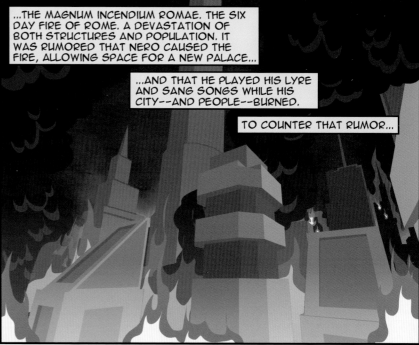

...THE MAGNUM INCENDIUM ROMAE. THE SIX DAY FIRE OF ROME. A DEVASTATION OF BOTH STRUCTURES AND POPULATION. IT WAS RUMORED THAT NERO CAUSED THE FIRE, ALLOWING SPACE FOR A NEW PALACE...

...AND THAT HE PLAYED HIS LYRE AND SANG SONGS WHILE HIS CITY--AND PEOPLE--BURNED.

TO COUNTER THAT RUMOR...

EVERYONE!

ON THE FLOOR!

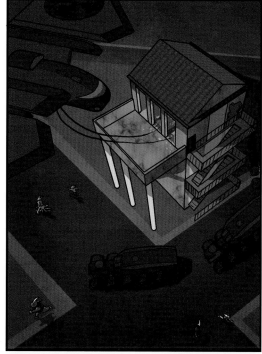

YOU!

I GET TO BE THE ONE TO ARREST YOU!

THE INFAMOUS PAUL, THE ROMAN JEW!

I'M GOING TO GET A BONUS FOR THIS!

ARRESTED, ONCE MORE.

THIS TIME, I KNEW.

THIS ARREST WOULD BE MY LAST.

THE VERDICT: GUILTY OF REBELLION! SEDITION! INCITATION!

THE SENTENCE: EXECUTION!

BEHEADING!

AND SO, HERE I AM...

EPILOGUE:

THE BIBLE DOES NOT TELL US EXACTLY HOW PAUL DIED, THOUGH EARLY CHURCH HISTORIANS SUCH AS EUSEBIUS WRITE THAT PAUL WAS EXECUTED BY EMPEROR NERO FOR TREASON. PAUL FEARLESSLY SPOKE OUT AGAINST THE EVILS OF THE WORLD AND DEFENDED THE NEW KINGDOM JESUS WOULD BUILD ON EARTH. THE MOST IMPORTANT PART OF PAUL'S STORY IS NOT WHEN OR HOW HE DIED, BUT HOW HE LIVED HIS LIFE FOR CHRIST! THOUGH HE FACED GREAT PERSECUTION, HE ALWAYS RELIED ON GOD TO GUIDE AND PROTECT HIM.

IN TODAY'S WORLD, FOLLOWERS OF JESUS STILL FACE VIOLENCE AND PERSECUTION. MANY PEOPLE HATE JESUS, AND THAT MEANS THEY MIGHT HATE US JUST BECAUSE WE FOLLOW HIM. DON'T BE AFRAID; JESUS HAS PREPARED US FOR THIS. HE STRENGTHENS US THROUGH TRIALS. PAUL WAS BULLIED, SPIT ON, HIT, AND EVEN THROWN IN JAIL FOR HIS FAITH, BUT HE ALWAYS LIVED A LIFE WORTHY OF THE GOSPEL. HE KEPT HIS EYES ON THE PRIZE—JESUS CHRIST!

NEVER GIVE UP OR LOSE SIGHT OF GOD WHEN THINGS GET ROUGH. WHEN YOU EXPERIENCE PERSECUTION, TEMPTATION, FRUSTRATION, OR HOPELESSNESS, TRY ASKING JESUS TO GIVE YOU THE SAME STRENGTH HE GAVE PAUL THROUGH THE HOLY SPIRIT. AND ALWAYS REMEMBER WHAT PAUL WROTE, "GOD IS FAITHFUL. HE WILL NOT ALLOW THE TEMPTATION TO BE MORE THAN YOU CAN STAND. WHEN YOU ARE TEMPTED, HE WILL SHOW YOU A WAY OUT SO THAT YOU CAN ENDURE." 1 CORINTHIANS 10:13 NLT

THE MISSIONARY JOURNEY OF PAUL

ROME
ADRIATIC SEA
MACEDONIA
THE BLACK SEA
PUTEOLI
AMPHIPOLIS PHILIPPI NEAPOLIS
THESSALONICA APOLLONIA
BEREA TROAS
RHEGIUM ASSOS ASIA
ANTIOCH OF PISIDIA
CILICIA
CORINTH ICONIUM
SYRACUSE CENCHREA ATHENS EPHESUS DERBE
MILETUS ATTALIA PERGA LYSTRA TARSUS
PATARA MYRA ANTIOCH
MALTA SALAMIS SELEUCIA
THE MEDITERRANEAN SEA PHOENIX FAIR HAVEN PAPHOS SYRIA
SIDON
TYRE
PTOLEMAIS
CAESAREA
JERUSALEM

KEY
— PAUL'S 1ST JOURNEY
— PAUL'S 2ND JOURNEY
— PAUL'S 3RD JOURNEY
— PAUL'S JOURNEY TO ROME

CHARACTER GLOSSARY

Before Paul the Apostle started following Jesus, he was known as Saul of Tarsus. He was a young Jewish Pharisee who was passionate about God and his Jewish faith. Saul saw the revolutionary movement of Jesus as a dangerous threat to Judaism.

Paul the Apostle is a real life superhero! Transformed from a ruthless persecutor of Christians to one of the bravest missionaries of all time, Paul is an excellent example for all of us to live by.

Barnabas was one of the first Christians in Jerusalem to befriend Paul. His name means "son of encouragement," which is a perfect description for such a kind-hearted man. We can learn a lot watching how Barnabas stuck by Paul's side when times got tough.

Stephen was the first Christian martyr, stoned to death for proclaiming his faith in the resurrected Christ. As death approached, Stephen called out for God to forgive his murderers. Saul stood by and watched.

Luke was one of Paul's best friends! He traveled with Paul on many of his journeys, fearlessly spreading the Good News of Jesus. Luke was also a medical doctor and a writer. He wrote the Gospel of Luke and the Book of Acts, which tells us the life story of Paul.

Ananias, a follower of Jesus, miraculously healed young Saul after he was blinded on the road to Damascus. God spoke to him in a dream and gave him specific orders to seek out and heal the man who had been hunting down Christians. That's some bold faith!

Peter was one of the first Christian leaders to accept Paul into his inner circle. He was one of the twelve apostles of Jesus. Peter was a faithful follower throughout his life and became one of the leaders of the early Church after Jesus' death and resurrection.

Timothy met Paul the Apostle during Paul's second missionary journey, and they became faithful friends. Paul mentored Timothy as he grew to become an important member of the early Church. He was a bold and brave defender of the faith.

MARIO DEMATTEO IS A STORYTELLER, A COMIC BOOK CREATOR, A POET, AND AN URBAN FARMER. IN 2014, MARIO'S WHOLE LIFE WAS FLIPPED UPSIDE DOWN WHEN HE INCURRED A PERMANENT SPINAL CORD INJURY, CONFINING HIM TO A WHEELCHAIR. THROUGH THE GRACE OF GOD, PERSEVERANCE, AN AMAZING FAMILY AND FRIENDS, AND A WHOLE LOT OF PRAYER, MARIO FOUND A CALLING IN COMIC BOOKS AND GRAPHIC NOVELS AS A POWERFUL WAY TO SPREAD LITERACY AND THE GOSPEL OF JESUS.

BEN AVERY IS A CHILDREN'S PASTOR BY DAY AND A COMIC BOOK WRITER BY NIGHT. A BELIEVER IN THE NEED FOR POSITIVE, ALL-AGES ENTERTAINMENT, BEN AVERY HAS WRITTEN OVER THIRTY GRAPHIC NOVELS FOR CHILDREN. BEN LIVES IN MISHAWAKA, INDIANA, WITH HIS WIFE AND FIVE CHILDREN.

MARK HARMON IS A PROFESSIONAL ILLUSTRATOR FOR CHILDREN'S BOOKS, COMICS, COMICS FOR KIDS, AND ANYTHING IN BETWEEN. HE CURRENTLY LIVES IN THE SMALL TOWN OF MOUNTAIN VIEW, WYOMING, WITH HIS WIFE AND THREE KIDS. MARK'S PROFESSIONAL CAREER STARTED AT THE AGE OF TEN WHEN HE WON A COLORING CONTEST. HE'S BEEN DRAWING EVER SINCE.